THE WORLD OF MYTHOLOGY

CHINESE MYTH

A TREASURY OF LEGENDS, ART, AND HISTORY

First published in North America in 2008 by M.E. Sharpe, Inc.

Sharpe Focus
An imprint of M.E. Sharpe, Inc.
80 Business Park Drive
Armonk, NY 10504
www.mesharpe.com

Copyright © 2008 Marshall Editions
A Marshall Edition
Conceived, edited, and designed by Marshall Editions
The Old Brewery, 6 Blundell Street, London N7 9BH, U.K.
www.quarto.com

Library of Congress Cataloging-in-Publication Data

Wilkinson, Philip.
   Chinese myth : a treasury of legends, art, and history / Philip Wilkinson.
       p. cm. -- (The world of mythology)
   Includes bibliographical references and index.
   ISBN 978-0-7656-8103-4 (hardcover : alk. paper)
   1. Mythology, Chinese--Juvenile literature. 2. Legends--China--Juvenile
literature. 3. China--Art--Juvenile literature. 4.
China--History--Juvenile literature. I. Title.

Originated in Hong Kong by Modern Age
Printed and bound in China by Midas Printing Limited

10 9 8 7 6 5 4 3 2 1

Publisher: Richard Green
Commissioning editor: Claudia Martin
Production: Nikki Ingram
Picture manager: Veneta Bullen
Design and editorial: Tall Tree Ltd.
Production: Anna Pauletti

Previous page: Fishermen wait on one of China's rivers at dusk.
This page and opposite: A golden lion stands guard in Beijing's Forbidden City, the old imperial palace.

THE WORLD OF MYTHOLOGY

CHINESE MYTH

A TREASURY OF LEGENDS, ART, AND HISTORY

PHILIP WILKINSON

Sharpe Focus

an imprint of M.E. Sharpe, Inc.

CONTENTS

CREATING THE UNIVERSE

THE GODS OF CHINESE LIFE

THE HEAVENLY EMPIRE

MYTHS OF BUDDHISM

INTRODUCTION

China is a huge country that stretches all the way from Central Asia in the west to the Yellow Sea in the east, a distance of some 2,500 miles (4,000 km). This vast area contains all kinds of countryside, from craggy mountains to lush river valleys, high plateaus to dense forests. This varied land gave birth to one of the richest cultures in the world—and one of the most vibrant collections of myths.

Over its long history, many people have made their homes in China, but because the country is cut off from most of its neighbors by mountains, deserts, and seas, the Chinese lived for thousands of years virtually isolated from the rest of the world. But despite this, China prospered, developing ways of growing foods such as wheat and rice that could thrive in a wide range of environments, and creating a unique civilization.

A UNIQUE CIVILIZATION

Many things about Chinese civilization were different from the cultures of the West. For example, the Chinese developed their own writing system, which is still in use, in which complex characters stand for whole words or ideas. Until the early twentieth century, the Chinese also had a very special system of government. At the top was the emperor, the senior member of a ruling family or dynasty and a person of supreme power. He wielded his authority through the world's first civil service, an enormous army of officials who got their jobs by passing an exam, and worked on behalf of the emperor in every area from tax-collection to organizing the building of bridges.

One of the most amazing facts about Chinese civilization is that the Chinese came up with many key inventions hundreds of years before they were thought of in the West. For instance, the Chinese were the inventors of gunpowder, porcelain, paper, and printing. They were among the first to develop metal casting. They made the first magnetic compass and the first suspension bridge. The wheelbarrow and the umbrella, the match and the kite, were all Chinese inventions.

Above: A traditional-style drawing from the Ming Dynasty (1368–1644) shows a figure sitting by a river in a typical Chinese landscape of rocks, trees, and mountains.

THE MYTHS

A sophisticated civilization first developed in China during the Shang Dynasty (c. 1600–1050 B.C.E.). Some of China's myths had probably already evolved by this time, spread by word of mouth. These traditional stories attempted to explain a host of difficult questions, such as how the world was created and why the land sometimes flooded. The myths featured numerous gods and goddesses who controlled elements of the natural world and helped China establish its civilization.

In the sixth century B.C.E., two new belief systems, Confucianism and Daoism (also known as Taoism), emerged in China. In the next few centuries, followers of these faiths wrote down the myths, sometimes altering them to fit their beliefs more closely, for example by inventing life stories for the many gods and goddesses. Still later, Chinese scholars of the Song Dynasty (960–1279 C.E.) recorded the myths more systematically, writing them down in reference books such as encyclopedias.

Confucianism and Daoism had a huge influence on the lives of China's people. Daoism was a religion developed by the sixth-century B.C.E. philosopher Laozi. It helped people to lead a better life and guided them along a path toward spiritual perfection. Confucianism was based on the work of the great thinker Confucius (551–479 B.C.E.).

Left: This seventeenth-century painting on silk shows the first Chinese emperor, Qin Shi Huangdi (chin-shee hwang-di) (221–210 B.C.E.), being carried by his servants. The emperor was such an important person that he was not expected to have to walk anywhere.

It emphasized the importance of family values and promoted a stable state and good government. In addition, China was also influenced by Buddhism, originally an Indian faith that developed in a special way when it was brought to China in the third century C.E.

These three belief systems combined to produce one of the most fascinating mythologies in the world. At its heart are stories about the immortals—the many godly beings who influence life on earth in all kinds of ways. The life of the immortals in many ways mirrors life on earth. The immortals are ruled by their own leader, the Jade Emperor, who has a court and a huge array of civil servants, just as the real emperor of China did.

The immortals did not belong to any one religion or belief system. Many have their origins in the time before Daoism or Confucianism emerged in China, while some date from the birth of those belief systems. Confucius encouraged the worship of some of the ancient gods and goddesses, while Laozi and the Daoists added to their ranks by introducing all kinds of other heroes who, when they died, were raised to the level of gods. Confucius himself was seen as a mortal man who became immortal after he died. In this way, the Chinese immortals are extremely diverse, ranging in character from the calm and merciful goddess Guan Yin (kwan yin) to the mischievous Monkey, who creates havoc wherever he goes.

There are also several different kinds of stories in Chinese mythology. One group of myths tells how the cosmos and human beings were created and deals with events—such as great floods and terrifying droughts—that happened in the early history of the human race. Another group recalls the deeds of China's so-called "culture heroes," the immortals who were said to have brought the distinctive aspects of the Chinese way of life to earth. Writing, agriculture, China's unique form of medicine, and Chinese civilization as a whole are all said to be the result of the work of specific immortals who gave the Chinese the tools or abilities they needed.

Many stories of the gods describe how they became immortals in the first place. Myths of this type relate the good deeds and special abilities that set these people apart from the rest of the human race, making it possible for them to join the Jade Emperor and other members of his court when they died. Many of these stories describe figures who now work to help human beings, and who respond to their prayers. Goddesses such as Zhunti Pusa (choon-tee poo-sah) and Guan Yin, for example, and immortals such as Amituo Fu (a-mi-to foo), are seen as the most merciful of the immortals, figures who will come to the help of people in need. In today's China, there are still people who offer them their prayers.

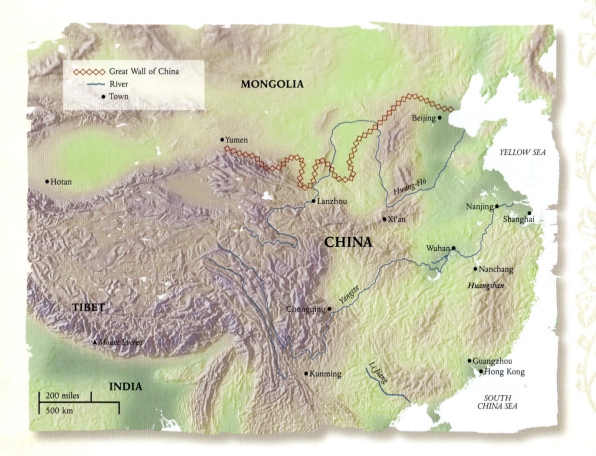

The Huang Shan (hwang shan) mountains tower above the Yangtze (yang-tsee) River in eastern China. Many myths offer explanations for the formation of such features of the Chinese landscape.

CREATING THE UNIVERSE

Some of the most famous Chinese myths tell the story of how the universe came into being and what happened after the creation. They describe a time when everything was a swirling, formless mass. The creator god, Pan Gu (pan goo), had the task of giving shape to this chaotic mass, bringing into being the features of the world as we know it, especially the features of the Chinese landscape: its trees, mountains, and long, winding rivers. But Pan Gu did not create the human race. People were an afterthought, created by a goddess, Nu Wa (nu wah), who molded them out of clay.

Alongside these stories are myths that tell of environmental disasters, especially flood and drought, events that are still common in China today. These legends belong with the creation myths both because they talk about events that happened very early in the history of the world and because afterward some parts of the world had to be re-created, as when the dragon-like character Yu dug new rivers to drain away the waters of the great flood.

THE CREATION OF THE WORLD

In the beginning there was no earth and no sky, no land and no oceans. Everything was swirling chaos, stretching endlessly in every direction, and all the elements—earth, water, fire, and air—were mixed together in an unruly mass that flowed continuously up and down and around and around. Gradually, the creator god, Pan Gu, came into being and began to give shape to the world.

It took thousands of years for Pan Gu to evolve, taking nourishment from the elements churning around him. And when the god did take his final form he was in a deep sleep, a sleep that lasted for thousands of years. As he slept, Pan Gu slowly gathered all the strength he would need to create the world.

PAN GU AWAKES

After sleeping for eighteen thousand years, Pan Gu awoke and looked this way and that. But it was dark, and he could not see very well. As his eyes adjusted to the gloom, all he could make out were the chaotic elements moving around him.

He was angry that he had come to life in such a chaotic, unpleasant world and, when he had gathered his immense strength, he hit out, delivering a violent blow as his great hand crashed onto the elements around him. There was an almighty boom that could have been heard millions of miles away—if there had been anyone alive to hear it.

As the crash echoed around the universe a miraculous thing happened. The elements of the cosmos, sent hurtling this way and that by Pan Gu's great blow, began to move in a less random way. The heavy things sank downward to form the rocks and soil of the earth, while the lighter elements floated upward to create the vast blue sky. Pan Gu had brought the two most important parts of the world into being.

This amazing act of creation did not happen instantly. The earth and sky kept growing. Every day the earth grew thicker and deeper, increasing in depth by more than a man's height each day and laying down layers of rock, heavy clay, and finer top soil.

Left: The creator god Pan Gu uses all his strength to hold the earth and the sky apart. One version of the myth of Pan Gu says that, in the beginning, the cosmos was in chaos, like a chicken's egg from which the creator emerges, as shown here.

At the same time, the sky grew ever higher and higher, expanding so that in the end even the great Pan Gu could not see its top.

Meanwhile, Pan Gu stood between earth and sky holding them apart with his enormous hands, preventing them from collapsing together again and turning back into the swirling chaos he had seen when he first woke. Just as the earth and sky grew, so did Pan Gu himself, adding to his height each day, and forcing the sky and earth farther and farther apart in the process.

For thousands of years Pan Gu stood like this, getting taller and taller and holding the earth and sky apart. At long last he felt sure that the earth and sky were so well separated that if he let go they would no longer collapse back into chaos. And so, exhausted and pleased with his work, he lay down on the ground to rest, and fell into a deep sleep.

THE BODY OF PAN GU

Pan Gu's sleep became deeper and deeper and his breathing became shallower and shallower until he died. But his death was not the end of creation, but a new beginning. As he breathed his last breaths, the air from his lungs traveled into the sky to become the winds and the clouds.

Creating the Universe

MYTHICAL BEASTS

A number of fantastic creatures appear in the myths of China. These exotic animals and birds often combine the features of more than one earthly creature. The phoenix, one of the creatures who guarded the heavenly empire of gods and goddesses, was among the most colorful. A beautiful bird, it was portrayed as a cross between an ornamental pheasant and a peacock, with one tail feather for each month of the year.

Perhaps the most famous of all Chinese mythical beasts were the dragons, scaly creatures that were said to live both in lakes (where they were the rulers of the fish, reptiles, and amphibians) and in the sky (where they pulled the chariots of some of the gods). Although they looked fearsome, the dragons of Chinese mythology were usually kind, and were said to bring wealth, good luck, and justice. Emperors often wore robes embroidered with dragons or had dragon decorations on their palaces, to show that they were just rulers.

Right: This phoenix, with its stunning, peacock-like tail, is embroidered on a silk robe worn by a Chinese empress of the nineteenth century. The beautiful design and golden threads in the robe would have made it stand out from the garments of the other people at the imperial court.

Right: Some of the walls and pavements in Beijing are decorated with dragons, like this one on the Nine Dragons Wall in the city's Beihai Park. The dragon design is made of ceramic tiles, which have been individually molded to show the churning green waves of the sea and the dragon's scaly body.

The last syllables from his lips joined the clouds in the sky to become the rumbling voice of the thunder. And the sweat that rolled from his body from all the effort at holding the earth and sky apart turned into the rain and dew that would refresh the earth, giving it back some of the energy he had spent. The god's two eyes became the sun and the moon, and the hairs from his beard joined them in the sky and were transformed into thousands of twinkling stars.

The vast body of Pan Gu became the mountain ranges that are scattered across the earth, and his hands and feet pointed to the four cardinal directions—the North and South Poles and the far eastern and western ends of the earth. The blood flowed from his veins to become the water in the world's rivers, and his flesh turned slowly into the fertile soil of the fields. Once the soil was in place, Pan Gu's hairs fell away, took root in the soil, and grew into the first flowers and trees.

And so Pan Gu finished his work of creation. He had brought into being a universe of stars and a beautiful earth, warmed by the sun, watered by the rain, and blessed with soil in which plants and trees could grow.

THE FIRST HUMANS

After Pan Gu had created the world, the other gods looked down on it. They admired Pan Gu's work, but one goddess, Nu Wa, felt that there was something missing. She decided to create a race of beings to people the earth. In this way the first humans were born.

The universe created by Pan Gu was a wonderful place. The earth took its place in a vast cosmos of thousands of stars that shone brightly at night. The moon's waxing and waning marked the months and years of the calendar. During the daytime, the sun shone, heating the air and the earth below.

In the warming sunlight and refreshing rain, life flourished on earth. Trees grew, dropping their seeds on the ground to produce saplings, which grew in turn, until huge areas were covered with thick forests. Smaller plants multiplied too, growing beautiful flowers that pleased the gods as they looked down on them. The rippling waters of the rivers and seas glinted in the sunlight.

Beasts of all kinds scampered through the woods and across the fields. They all found places to live, whether in the trees, in the fields, or in holes in the ground. And a whole race of creatures, from fish and eels to crabs and starfish, swam in the rivers and seas. The gods were pleased with the universe, and impressed that Pan Gu had made such a wonderful world.

A MAN OF CLAY

But one goddess, Nu Wa—although she admired the creation just as much as the others did—thought that the world could be improved. Nu Wa was one of the most striking of all the deities who ruled the heavens. Unlike most of the gods and goddesses, who looked very much like humans, Nu Wa had the head of a woman but the body of a serpent. She was destined to change the story of the world forever.

Nu Wa's human-like eyes gave her good eyesight, and she could see far and wide across the earth. Although the world was filled with beautiful mountains and rivers,

THE EARLY PEOPLE OF CHINA

The earliest Chinese state was formed under the rulers of the Shang Dynasty, who came to power in around 1600 B.C.E. and ruled until about 1050 B.C.E. The Shang people built China's first towns and cities, including a famous capital city at Anyang. Above all, the Shang people were famous for their metalwork. They knew how to heat rocks to extract the metal ore and, using the bronze they made in this manner, they developed a way of making beautiful objects by heating the metal until it melted and pouring it into molds. Many of the metal objects that they made were used in religious rituals.

Right: This Shang Dynasty wine vessel is in the form of a highly decorated elephant. The creature's body is covered with designs representing clouds and thunder, while the tip of the trunk supports a crouching tiger and the head of a phoenix.

with great forests and vast seas, to Nu Wa it seemed strangely empty. When she visited earth she felt lonely and she thought the world would be a better place, and more interesting to the gods, if it was populated with a new kind of creature.

The goddess thought about this problem for a long time, and then she began to search the earth for what she needed. She had noticed that, although many parts of the world were covered with water, sand, or hard rocks, some areas were covered with soft, flexible clay. The goddess realized that she could use this clay to make things.

Chinese Myth

So she went to one of the places where the ground was made of clay—and searched the place for the kind of yellowish clay that is easy to mold into all kinds of different shapes.

Picking up a lump of clay in her dragon-like claws, Nu Wa began to mold and model like a sculptor until she had produced a figure.

The creature that Nu Wa molded out of the clay had a head similar to her own but, instead of a dragon's or serpent's body, it had two legs and a pair of arms—Nu Wa had made a human figure. But Nu Wa's clay man was different from the figures made by sculptors: when she placed him on the ground, he came to life.

PEOPLING THE EARTH

Nu Wa was overjoyed, and began to laugh as her creation started to jump around and dance as if he were trying to entertain her. She was so pleased that she soon made some more humans—both men and women—and smiled to herself as they jumped and danced about in front of her. She realized that she had added the finishing touch to creation, and had completed the enormous job that had been begun by the great creator god Pan Gu.

Soon the humans began to explore the earth and to find different places all over the planet's surface where they could make their homes. They seemed happy, and whenever Nu Wa came to earth she was pleased to see them. The goddess was no longer lonely on her visits to earth.

But after some years had passed, Nu Wa saw that her human creations were beginning to get old. She realized that, unlike the gods, they would one day die. So the goddess gave humanity a new power: the ability to have children. She taught them the ways of marriage, and soon the planet was alive with new sounds—the cries of babies and the noise of children playing. It made the goddess happy, and she saw that the people were happy, too.

Now there would be an endless supply of humans, who could care for the planet, bring up the next generation of children, and entertain the gods and goddesses whenever they decided to visit their planet.

Left: The goddess Nu Wa, who molded the human race out of clay, had the head of a woman but the body of a dragon or serpent. She gave humanity the power to have children and people the world.

The Land of China

China is a vast country, covering more than 3.6 million square miles (9.3 million sq km). Its scenery ranges from the high mountains of the Himalayas to the plains of the east. It is also home to some of the world's longest rivers. Many of China's myths describe this huge land, telling of its creation and how the immortals taught the skills of agriculture. China's size also explains why there are such a large number of myths—the country has been home to many different peoples, who developed different stories over the years.

Above: At the busiest times of the farming year, everyone in the area came to help. This thirteenth- or fourteenth-century C.E. picture depicts the rice harvest.

RIVERS

The rivers of China are among its people's most important resources. The major rivers have been used for transport for centuries. Rivers are also a vital source of fish for food and for water to irrigate the fields. However, the rivers are also dangerous. The vast volumes of water carried by the Yangtze, for example, have led to frequent floods.

Right: A man on a raft crosses the Li River (or Li Jiang) in China's southern province of Guangxi. The area's craggy uplands are visible in the background.

Left: Mist forms around the upper slopes of the Yellow Mountains (or Huangshan). Chinese myths frequently portray mountains as places of mystery.

MOUNTAINS

A large portion of China is upland country, and there are many mountains, especially in western and central China. The Chinese creation myth tells how the mountain ranges were formed out of the body of the creator god Pan Gu. Chinese people see mountains as special, often holy, places, where pilgrims flock to temples or where people go to be alone and contemplate nature.

FARMING

Agriculture was vital to provide a food supply for China's huge population. One of the key crops was rice, which grows especially well in the fertile south of the country, especially on either side of the Yangtze River. According to mythology, it was the god Shen Nong who taught China's people how to farm.

Above: China has many large lakes that are home to all kinds of wildlife, including wading birds such as the white crane. This one appears on the badge of a high-ranking civil servant of the seventeenth century C.E. But this beautiful bird, which could fly for long distances, had a special meaning in Chinese mythology. It was said to be a messenger of the gods and the creature that carried the souls of the dead to the Western Paradise.

THE TEN SUNS

In the beginning there was not one sun but ten. Usually they took turns to shine in the sky, but one day they all decided to shine at once. A blistering heat fell on the earth and there was terrible suffering. The emperor of China, Yao (yow), did not know what to do to save humanity from this catastrophe.

Long ago there were ten boys, each of whom shone with a dazzling light. Some said they were the sons of the Emperor of Heaven; others that they were the children of an immortal called Di Jun. The ten boys lived in a great tree, which towered above the Eastern Ocean. The tree was so vast that people said that one thousand men, all with their arms stretched out, could not hold hands around its enormous trunk. The branches of this tree stretched so high into the sky that people on earth could not see their tips.

Every dawn, one of the boys took off from the top of this vast tree and flew slowly across the sky, lighting up the world until he finally came to rest on the tree again at nighttime. In this way, each child was a sun. Each day a different sun shone in the sky, as the ten boys took their turn. The people on earth did not realize that there was more than one sun, because each appeared in turn and no two ever came out at the same time. The people loved the suns because they brought warmth and comfort, and they helped their food plants to ripen.

DROUGHT AND DEVASTATION

All went well with the ten suns until one terrible day. No one knows why, but the ten suns decided to come out and shine at once. First the sky brightened as normal, then another sun came out and it got much hotter, and then another and another. By the time all ten suns were out, the earth was drying up, the crops were dying, and even the rivers were beginning to evaporate. There was no rain, both people and cattle went thirsty, fires raged through the forests, and soon people began to die.

Above: A rubbing taken from a carved stone relief of the second century B.C.E. shows the archer Yi shooting the suns, who are depicted in the form of birds perching in a tree.

But the heat was not the only problem. As the earth and the air heated up, more strange things began to happen. People brought reports to Emperor Yao of monsters that were appearing in different places in China. One messenger described a creature with a man's body, an animal's head, and a single, deadly, razor-sharp fang. Another described a giant peacock beating its wings together and causing powerful gales. A third messenger told Yao how a sea monster was devouring fishermen and travelers on China's rivers and lakes.

THE SUPREME RULER SENDS HELP

Emperor Yao, who could usually solve any problem that he faced, was baffled. What could he do to stop this terrible, burning heat and destroy these fearsome creatures? He prayed to the Supreme Ruler. The ruler heard Yao's prayers and decided to send his most skillful warrior, the archer Yi (yee), to help. Yi arrived on earth at nighttime, when the full moon was shining in the sky. The suns had gone to rest in their tree for a few

WEAPONS

Although Yi's preferred weapon was the bow, the Chinese developed many other weapons early in their history. Their skill in metalwork, for example, enabled them to create all kinds of knives and swords in bronze, and examples survive from as early as the seventh century B.C.E., some with finely decorated handles. In the same period they also used the battle axe and the halberd—a bronze blade mounted on a long bamboo pole. A halberd was a fearsome weapon when swung by a Chinese charioteer. But even more impressive, and powerful over long distances, was the crossbow. The Chinese invented this weapon some time before 450 B.C.E., centuries before it appeared in Europe.

hours, but they would soon be out again and increase the unbearable suffering on earth. Yi went straight to the imperial palace to find out what Yao needed him to do.

Yao was impressed with Yi and his great red bow, but doubted whether a bow and arrows were strong enough weapons against the ten suns that would rise in the morning. Yi decided to show the emperor the power of his bow. He loosed an arrow high into the sky and the pair watched as it traveled for miles, eventually splitting in two the trunk of a tall pine tree on top of a mountain in the far distance. The emperor began to hope that Yi might be able to save his people from drought and death after all.

Yao could not sleep through the night from too much worrying and instead spent his time praying to the Supreme Ruler. A little while before dawn, Yao left his room in the palace and went to get Yi. He was already awake, too, quietly waiting for the dawn.

Together, the pair walked through the streets of the capital city. Yao explained to Yi that he wanted to take him to the tallest watchtower on the eastern city wall, where the archer would get a good view of the suns as they came up. When the tower's watchman saw them coming, he was worried that two people should be out so early. But when he saw that one was the emperor, he bowed low and let them pass. Yao and Yi climbed the steps of the watchtower in silence.

Opposite: Archery was an important skill for Chinese warriors. They practiced bowmanship and held archery contests even as recently as the eighteenth century C.E., as shown on this painting, done on a piece of silk.

YI FIRES HIS ARROWS

As the sky in the east began to turn yellow with the dawn, Yi chose ten arrows, all tipped with pin-sharp bronze arrowheads, and loaded them into his quiver. No sooner did he have his arrows ready than a procession of ten suns appeared over the horizon. Straight away Yi felt the air heat up and saw some clumps of dry grass in a distant field begin to smolder. He knew he had to act quickly—and immediately lifted his bow and let loose his first arrow. In seconds, one of the ten suns disappeared and a great black crow, the spirit of the sun, fell to the ground.

Yao was impressed, but there were still nine suns, and already the heat was unbearable. Yi wasted no time. Again and again he raised his bow to the east, and one after another, the crow-like sun spirits fell to the ground defeated. Yi seemed to be enjoying his task and, as he brought down the sixth sun, Yao realized that there were still four arrows left. Would Yi forget and shoot down all ten suns, plunging the earth into total darkness?

While Yi was aiming at the seventh sun, Yao crept quickly up behind the archer and silently removed an arrow from the quiver, hiding it in his sleeve. Yi shot his remaining arrows, removing nine of the ten suns and leaving one left to warm the earth. Soon clouds formed in the sky and life-giving rain began to fall again. The terrible time of drought was over.

MONSTERS OF THE LAND, AIR, AND WATER

But there was still the threat of the monsters that rampaged through the land, air, and water. Could Yi defeat those too? For days, Yi stalked the monster with the deadly fang. Eventually he came to a place where the ground was littered with severed human heads—he had found the spot where the creature decapitated its human enemies before devouring their bodies. Suddenly, Yi saw a movement as the beast emerged from a nearby cave, its body concealed behind a huge shield. Yi drew an arrow and stood ready to shoot, daring the monster to come closer. The beast advanced toward him, but was still hidden by the shield. As the creature got within a few feet of Yi, it dropped its shield to pounce on the bowman. In a split-second, Yi shot his arrow, aiming at the beast's gum. The terrible tooth broke off and pierced the throat of the creature, which dropped dead on the ground.

Next Yi chased down the giant peacock. The archer thought that one arrow might not be enough to kill the great bird, so he tied a cord to his arrow before he fired. When the arrow entered the bird's flesh, Yi gave a mighty pull on the end of the cord and the bird flapped its wings to try to escape. To and fro the pair pulled, and it seemed likely that Yi would tire first. But with one last great effort Yi gave an enormous tug, brought the bird to the ground, and cut off its head with his sword.

Finally Yi went to the lake where the sea monster was lurking. He borrowed a fishing boat, sailed to the center of the lake, and waited for the monster to appear. Sure enough, the creature's scaly back soon started to rise out of the water. Yi aimed and shot, but the pain caused by the arrow only made the monster thrash around, making the waters more and more turbulent and threatening to capsize Yi's boat. The waters were so rough that Yi could not keep steady enough to aim.

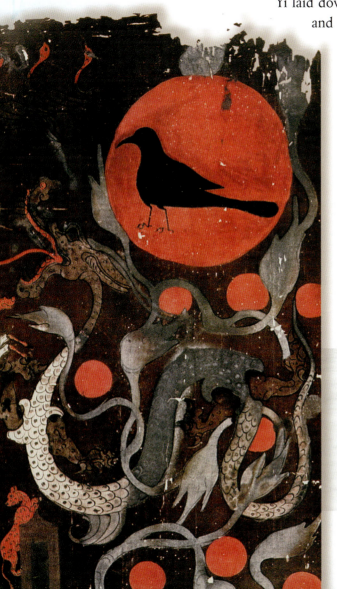

Yi laid down his bow in the bottom of the boat and looked down into the water. As the little craft crashed against the waves, Yi jumped, diving deep toward the sea serpent's scale-covered back. Time and again Yi stabbed the monster's body with his sword. Time and again the beast turned and tried to grasp Yi in its wide jaws. But at last Yi lodged his blade deep in the creature's flesh. The serpent fell lifeless to the lake bed, and Yi swam to the surface gasping for air.

As the sun dropped toward the western horizon, Yi floated to the shore of the lake and lay down for a long, well-earned rest.

Left: Because the sun traveled across the sky each day, the Chinese saw it as a bird that flew through the air. In one myth, the bird, a crow, carries the sun to the top of a tree before taking off on its daily journey through the sky. But other stories—and paintings like this one from about 190 B.C.E.—portray the crow as living inside the sun's disc.

Creating the Universe

THE GREAT FLOOD

There came a time when the Emperor of Heaven was angry with the men and women on earth, because of their wicked ways. He sent the water spirit Kong-kong to make a great flood to punish humanity. Soon the rivers broke their banks and the whole surface of the earth was covered in water. Men and women had to build nests in tall trees in order to survive. With the fields waterlogged, there was nothing to eat.

When he saw the terrible flood, Kun (koon), the grandson of the Emperor of Heaven, took pity on the human race. He knew that among the treasures of the Heavenly Emperor's palace was a kind of soil that absorbed water and could turn lakes and rivers into dry land. Kun took some of the precious soil from the palace and traveled to earth. Then Kun began to spread the soil out on the flooded plains and along the river valleys. The soil absorbed the water and soon, where there had been floods, there was dry land; and where there had been deep lakes, there were marshes.

The people were overjoyed by what Kun had done. They came down from their tree-top refuges and began to rebuild their damaged houses and replant their sodden fields. It seemed as if human life would be able to go on as it had before the great flood.

THE EMPEROR OF HEAVEN'S REVENGE

But Kun had stopped the flood without asking the permission of his grandfather, the Emperor of Heaven. This made the Emperor as furious with Kun as he had been with the people of the earth. He sent more rains to make conditions on earth even worse and commanded the fire spirit Zhu Rong (choo jung) to search out Kun and murder him.

But when Zhu Rong stabbed Kun's body with his sword and killed him, an extraordinary thing happened. Kun's body did not decay like a human body does when a person dies. Instead it remained looking just as it did when Kun had been alive. This was because Kun was an immortal. While Kun's body lay there, a new being was coming to life inside.

CHINA'S CHANGEABLE RIVERS

Many of China's rivers, including both the Yangtze and the Yellow (Huang-Ho) rivers, run from the high mountains of western China to the plains of the east. They collect vast amounts of water from the uplands, and if the snow melts suddenly or there is heavy rain, the rivers can flood, causing the destruction of crops and homes, and even loss of life.

Due to the threat of flooding, the people of China have been building canals, dykes, and other flood-control measures for hundreds of years. The effort to control flooding continues today with huge engineering projects to build dams, such as an enormous new one near the Three Gorges on the Yangtze River.

Left: The enormous power of China's rivers is clear, as here at Hukou in Jixian county, when water crashes over the rocks at weirs and waterfalls.

夏禹長於地理脈泉知陰隨時設防退為肉刑

Left: This portrait of Yu includes an inscription that tells how he was skilled in mapping the earth, recording water sources, and building dykes. In the picture he carries a tool that was used for dredging.

The Emperor of Heaven saw Kun's body and realized that he had not died in the normal way. So he sent another spirit, armed with a sharp sword, to finish off the unfortunate Kun.

The spirit found Kun, took aim, and struck the body with his sword. The sharp blade sliced through Kun's flesh—but instead of blood pouring out, a young dragon emerged out of the corpse. The dragon opened its wings and flew straight to the court of the Emperor of Heaven.

THE WORK OF YU

When the dragon arrived at the Emperor's court he announced that he was Yu, son of Kun, and he begged the Emperor to save humanity by allowing him to put a stop to the floods. In spite of his former anger, the Emperor was moved by Yu's plea, and thought that perhaps humanity had suffered long enough at the hands of Kong-kong. After some deliberation, the Emperor agreed to Yu's request. Yu immediately stretched his wings and set out for earth. He took with him a load of the special soil that Kun had used previously to soak up water and put a stop to the floods.

When Yu arrived he found that earth was totally under the control of Kong-kong. He had turned the roads into rivers, the fields into lakes, the rivers into raging torrents, and the lakes into stormy seas. Furious, Yu landed on top of a tall mountain, called all the spirits together around him, and showed them the havoc that Kong-kong had created. The spirits were so shocked that they surrounded Kong-kong and chased him far away from the earth.

Then Yu set to work to tame the floods and bring down the water level. He raised new mountain ranges and laid out fields where men and women could grow their crops. And he built drainage dykes and new rivers to take away the excess water, marking out their course on the land with his tail. The people saw that the country's great mountain ranges and the long rivers such as the Yangtze and Yellow rivers were the results of Yu's efforts as he worked hard to banish the floods from the country. It took him some thirty years to tame the floods and make all these new features so that the land was fit for humans again.

The water spirit Kong-kong had vanished from China and no one in heaven or on earth had any idea where he had gone. But even today, when it has rained very hard or after there have been heavy snows, China's rivers sometimes burst their banks. When this happens, men and women have to work as hard as Yu to drain away the water, clean the mud from their houses, and banish the spirit of the floods.

A textile of the Qing (ching) Dynasty, made in around 1800 C.E., shows groups of immortals gathering against a backdrop of mountains and trees. The Qing ruled China from 1644 to 1912.

The Gods of Chinese Life

Ancient China had a very advanced civilization that was different from any culture in the West. The Chinese created many inventions, from metalworking to silk weaving, long before they were known in the rest of the world. These inventions were made so long ago that even the Chinese did not know the names of the inventors. So to explain how these technologies came about, they told stories about how skills such as farming and metalworking were handed down to humans by the gods and goddesses.

These deities are sometimes called the "culture heroes" of China, because they showed people how to make the advances that set China apart from the world's other cultures. There was one god, Fu Xi (foo hsi), who devised China's unique form of writing, and a number of physician gods, such as Yao Wang (yow wang) and Wu Tao (woo tow), who showed the Chinese their special medical skills using acupuncture and herbs. Even today, some people in remote Chinese communities may take home an image of Wu Tao from their local temple to help a family member recover from an illness.

BRINGERS OF CIVILIZATION

Three of the immortals kept a special eye on men and women and helped them develop many of the skills they needed in order to survive and prosper. These were the three "culture heroes" Fu Xi, Shen Nong, and Huang Di (hwang dee), and they had an enormous impact on humanity, helping the men and women of China build the great civilization for which their country became famous.

After the goddess Nu Wa had created humanity, she married the god Fu Xi. Like Nu Wa, he had the body of a dragon but a head like that of a man. Fu Xi had such great knowledge, in so many different fields, that he could have founded civilization on his own.

Many of Fu Xi's inventions were inspired by the natural world. The god looked at the things around him and imitated them. The first gift he gave people was fire, which he found out about by looking at the natural fires that started in forests when lightning struck the trees. He soon discovered how to make fire by rubbing pieces of wood together. He then taught men and women how to do this, so that they could keep warm and cook food. Not long afterward, while watching a spider spinning her web, Fu Xi invented the fishing net, and gave people a whole new source of food from the rivers and seas.

Coming up with inventions and discoveries like fire and fishing nets made Fu Xi realize how important the natural world could be. The world was full of rich resources that people could use, from the sky, which could tell you what the weather was going to be like, to the ground, which was where food plants grew. The more the god thought about these things, the more he realized that it would be useful to find some way of describing the world, so that people could make a lasting record of its wonders.

So it was that Fu Xi came up with China's first writing system, the *ba gua* (pah gwah), or eight trigrams. The trigrams were a series of symbols, each made up of three lines drawn in different ways. Some said that Fu Xi invented the trigrams after listening to the voices of the eight winds blowing across the countryside. But in reality he devised eight symbols because he wanted each symbol to stand for something important in the universe. There was a symbol for heaven, one for earth, one for water, one for fire, one for mountains, one for storm, one for wind, and, finally, one for marshland.

These eight symbols were the beginnings of a system of writing that grew and grew in complexity until the people of China could eventually use it to describe everything around them—not to mention all kinds of ideas and beliefs. But the trigrams were not just symbols. The *ba gua* also had magical powers, and people who understood them could use them to predict the future. Fu Xi had created one of the most powerful tools that the Chinese people used to build their civilization.

SHEN NONG

By following the example of Fu Xi, with his skill at looking at the natural world, people learned how to find plants that they could eat and to locate drinking water in rivers and streams. But there was a problem. It was not always easy to find good food plants.

Sometimes people tried to eat plants that did not taste good, or even species that were poisonous. Many people suffered and some even died because they chose the wrong food.

The farmer god, Shen Nong, helped people to solve this problem. He showed people several different grains that they could sow in the ground and then harvest. He also taught people about the qualities of the soil: which soils were the most fertile, which were barren, which soils were well drained, and which were too wet or dry to grow crops. With all this new knowledge, people were able to become farmers. They could control their own food supply, and there were fewer deaths by starvation or poisoning. Villages began to prosper and grow in China as never before.

Like Fu Xi, Shen Nong was famous for his knowledge of the natural world. As time went by, people began to ask him if there were any new food plants they could grow or gather, to make their diet more varied. They were scared to try different plants without his advice, because some of them could be poisonous.

Left: Much of the land in China is made up of hills and mountains, where it is difficult to find enough flat land on which to grow crops. In some areas, as here in present-day Yunnan province, people cut away the sloping land to make narrow, flat terraces where they can grow wheat.

Shen Nong decided to help the people by personally testing all the plants that grew in China. He found out which were bitter and which were sweet and good to eat. He discovered which were safe and which were poisonous. Because he was an immortal, the poisonous plants could not kill Shen Nong—but they could still make him feel ill. There were so many plants to taste that in one day alone he was made ill seventy times because of all the poison he ate. Shen Nong passed on all the information he learned to the men and women of China, so soon they had the most varied and enjoyable diet in the world, with all kinds of fruits, leaves, and roots that were in season at different times of the year. But it was still hard work growing all these good foods, because the farmers needed to do a great deal of digging to prepare the soils for their crops.

So Shen Nong gave China's farmers one last gift. He invented the plow so that people would be able to turn the soil easily. Farming was still hard work, but it was no longer so backbreaking, and the people of China had time to enjoy all the wonderful fruit and vegetables that Shen Nong had helped them to cultivate.

THE REAL FIRST EMPEROR

Since they were so powerful and had such a huge impact on life in China, the three bringers of civilization are often known in China as "emperors." But Fu Xi and Shen Nong were in fact gods who came down to earth to look after humanity, while Qin Shi Huang Di (meaning "emperor") was a real man who ruled China between 221 and 207 B.C.E. He was the first person to unify the country into a single state and is known as the Shi Huang Di, meaning "first emperor."

Shi Huang Di achieved a lot during his short reign, introducing standard weights and measures, forming an enormous army, building parts of the Great Wall, and constructing a huge tomb for himself, complete with its famous army of life-size terracotta soldiers. To do all this he needed money, so he taxed people heavily, which meant that many of his subjects suffered under his rule and some even died of starvation. But later people honored him because of his achievements in unifying the country. After he died, they saw him as the immortal who brought the first true civilization to China.

帝 皇 始 秦

Above: The surviving pictures of Qin Shi Huang Di, like this seventeenth-century C.E. woodcut, date from long after his lifetime, so no one knows exactly what he looked like. He is always shown as an imposing, bearded figure.

HUANG DI

The last of the three mythical bringers of Chinese civilization was Huang Di, the Yellow Emperor. He was said to be the first man to rule all of China and he was known as the Yellow Emperor because his character and reign were associated with the element of earth, which was usually portrayed in a yellow color. Unlike Fu Xi and Shen Nong, Huang Di was not born a god but a mortal.

Yet Huang Di had a miraculous beginning. His mother became pregnant after she saw lightning strike a star, and Huang Di was born a full twenty months later. When he grew up he had to fight many enemies in a series of bitter wars but eventually took control of the whole of China.

China's civilization made huge advances during the reign of Huang Di. The scholars at his court invented instruments for looking at the moon and stars, and the observations they made enabled them to work out China's first method of calculating time and the calendar. The arts of pottery and woodworking were perfected during Huang Di's reign, and China prospered. Huang Di was seen as the father of the great civilization that developed in China over the following millennia.

Huang Di ruled China for around a hundred years, before dying at the amazing age of 111. When he died his body was seen on the back of a dragon, which flew up into the sky, climbing so high that it eventually disappeared. When his people saw this, they realized that Huang Di was going to join the gods in heaven. He was the first human being to become an immortal.

Right: Qin Shi Huang Di's tomb is one of the wonders of China. It contains more than 7,000 life-size statues of soldiers, each one modeled as an individual portrait of one of Shi Huang Di's men. The statues originally carried real weapons, but many of these were removed by tomb-robbers.

Life in Ancient China

Largely isolated from the rest of the world, the ancient Chinese empire developed its own way of life. As well as coming up with many inventions, the Chinese developed unique methods of building and their own style of costume. Some of the products of this ancient way of life, such as the famous Great Wall, survive today.

Right: This twelfth-century drawing shows both traditional Chinese buildings, with their upturned tile roofs, and various forms of transport. As well as carts and wheelbarrows, people transported goods using baskets balanced on shoulder-poles, while the wealthy rode on horseback or were carried in a comfortable sedan chair.

INVENTIONS

The dozens of inventions that the Chinese came up with ranged across all kinds of fields, from engineering to medicine. They were making steel some 2,000 years before anyone in the West. Chinese doctors knew about the circulation of the blood 1,800 years before their counterparts in the West.

Left: This fourteenth-century C.E. illustration shows a pump designed to raise water from a river to the fields. Although it is a practical machine, it has a mythological name—the dragon's backbone—perhaps because to the first people who saw it, it seemed to work by magic.

WRITING

China developed its own system of writing, using thousands of different symbols, each representing a whole word or idea. The first Chinese writing to survive dates from the Shang Dynasty (c. 1600–1050 B.C.E.). In ancient China, few men or women could read or write except for highly educated people. The best jobs were in the employ of the emperor in China's huge civil service. The first civil servants were appointed at the beginning of the Han Dynasty, in around 206 B.C.E. To get a job in the civil service, you had to pass an exam, so all civil servants could read and write.

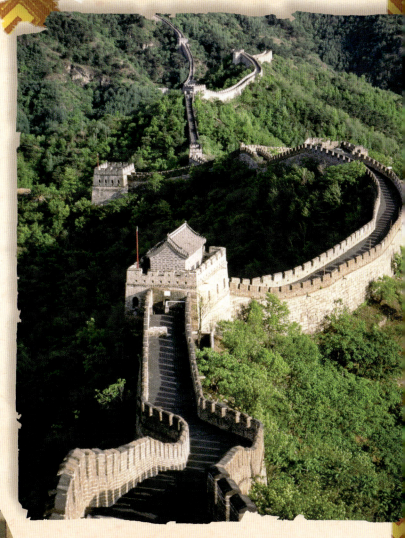

Above: By the fourth century B.C.E., the rulers of China were building walls to protect their territory and keep out invading nomads from the north and west. Over the centuries, the emperors added to these walls and joined them up to make the vast Great Wall, which stretched for thousands of miles along the country's borders.

Left: Scribes had to be able to master calligraphy, or beautiful writing, which the Chinese considered to be one of the most important art forms. To write the thousands of Chinese characters well required years of practice.

LEARNING TWO NEW SKILLS

Two of the most valuable skills of the Chinese people—metalworking and silk production—came to the country long before they reached other parts of the world. The ability to make items out of metal and the technique of producing soft, fine silk cloth set China apart. It was the mighty warrior Chi You (chee yoo) who first discovered the skills of metalworking, while the secrets of silk production were revealed by a creature known as Can Nu.

Chi You was a fearsome-looking creature with the head and horns of a bull. He was incredibly strong—so strong that people said his head was made of bronze and his brows of iron.

He had a group of followers, made up of his seventy-two brothers, and they were all powerful and fearless like Chi You himself. They could build up their strength still more by eating pebbles and they could all do terrible damage to their enemies by simply butting them with their enormous heads.

One day there was an earthquake and one of China's tallest mountains, Ko Lu, burst open. Great rocks fell everywhere and at first water rushed out of the cracks in the stone, as underground streams found a new route into the open air. But then a strange new substance appeared from within the mountain.

The strange new material was metal. The warrior Chi You went to the mountain to see this substance that everyone was talking about. He soon saw that the metal could be used to form useful objects—and that this could be incredibly helpful to humankind. Naturally, the warrior's first thought was to use the metal to make weapons, and soon he was showing people how to make swords, spears, and lances, as well as strong protective armor.

Chinese Myth

Above: One result of the Chinese skill in metalwork was that they discovered that a magnetized piece of iron would point north–south. The Chinese invented the magnetic compass in around the fourth century B.C.E., over a thousand years before it appeared in Europe.

People quickly caught on and soon they all had swords to brandish against their enemies and armor to defend themselves. They realized that they could use metal tools in peacetime, too. Knives, hoes, and even plowshares made of metal were the result. Thanks to Chi You, China was able to become one of the most advanced civilizations in the world.

Chi You lived at the time of the Yellow Emperor, Huang Di, and was jealous of the power of the great ruler. He decided to stage a revolt. He gathered together his brothers and declared war on the emperor. There were several hard-fought battles.

THE SECRET OF SILK

The Chinese were the first people in the world to discover how to make silk from fibers collected from the cocoons of silk moths. The process of harvesting the fibers, weaving the cloth, cleaning it, and decorating it, was a long one, but people thought it was worth it because the finished cloth was so luxurious and beautiful. The fabric was reserved for the upper classes: the emperor and his court, the rich, and high-ranking officials. They prized it both for its softness and for the way it could be beautifully decorated.

When the Chinese began to trade with the West in around 500 B.C.E., they sent cargoes of silk by camel on the so-called Silk Road to the Mediterranean. The Silk Road was a network of thousands of miles of commonly traveled trade routes linking cities and markets. Westerners paid huge prices for the silk, and the Chinese were careful to keep secret the way it was made. The secrets of how silk was produced were first known outside China in around 500 C.E., when craft workers in Constantinople (present-day Istanbul) began to make the cloth. But the Chinese still produced more silk, and of better quality, so the trade carried on for centuries more.

Left: This silk robe of the late nineteenth century C.E. is made of the finest silk and richly decorated with embroidery. A high-quality garment such as this must have been worn by a rich woman.

Many times it looked as if Chi You and his brothers would win, because of their incredible strength and because Chi You could create dense fogs to confuse his enemies.

But both sides were armed with metal weapons and so Chi You's invention did not give him the advantage over Huang Di. After a long struggle, the emperor was actually victorious. Eventually people were able to forgive Chi You for the chaos caused by his revolt, because he had given them such a useful ability in the art of metalworking.

THE HORSE'S MARRIAGE

Silk came to China after a man had to leave home for a long trip on business. His daughter missed him sorely. One day when she was grooming her horse, she said that she would marry anyone who brought her father back home. In an instant, the horse bolted out of the stable and out of sight.

The horse galloped as far as the town where the girl's father was staying. When the man saw the creature he thought some mishap might have happened to his family, so rode back home straight away. The girl was overjoyed that her horse had brought her father back home, and the father was relieved to see his family unharmed.

But although the girl gave her horse extra fodder as a reward, the animal seemed unhappy, leaving most of the food and neighing loudly whenever she came near. Then the father realized what had happened: the horse had heard what the girl had said and wanted to marry her.

The father thought he would put an end to that idea by killing the horse, and soon the poor animal lay dead on the ground. But as the girl was looking sadly at her horse's body, the animal's skin came to life, wrapped itself around her, and took off into the sky!

The next day, the girl's parents saw a strange, caterpillar-like creature with a head like a horse's hanging in a nearby tree. This was their daughter, who had become Can Nu, or "Lady Silkworm," and she showed them the fine thread that she could produce. Soon the girl's mother and father had gathered the thread and discovered how to make it into the finest cloth anyone had ever seen. They had lost their daughter, but had gained one of the most priceless skills known to the people of China.

Left: This twelfth-century C.E. painting shows women pounding newly woven silk cloth to prepare it for dyeing.

LESSONS OF THE
DRAGON KING

Sun Simiao (soon si-mi-ow) was a great healer. He loved the countryside because it was a good source of medicinal plants. He knew at a glance how to recognize the plants that had healing properties. He also liked to talk to an old hermit who lived in a lonely spot and who told him many more secrets of the healer's art.

One day Sun was walking in the countryside looking for plants when he came across a shepherd who was trying to kill a small blue snake by hitting it with his stick. Sun could not bear to see the innocent creature harmed so he told the shepherd to stop. At first the shepherd refused to stop beating the snake as he thought the poisonous creature would harm him or his flocks.

Sun was so sorry for the snake that he offered the shepherd his clothes in return for the animal's freedom. Finally the shepherd agreed, and Sun picked up the snake and carried it off. He tended the animal carefully, treating its wounds with healing herbs until one day it was strong enough to slither off into the undergrowth.

AN AUDIENCE WITH THE DRAGON KING

Sun returned to his wanderings once more. On the road he met some horsemen who told him about the beautiful city they were traveling to. They said that Sun would be made welcome there. Sun decided to join the horsemen, and when he reached the city he was taken into a huge palace and told he would be introduced to the king. When he entered the great audience hall he saw the king sitting on a throne. Next to him stood a small boy dressed in blue robes.

"Thank you for saving the life of my son," said the king. "I am the Dragon King and my son and I have the power to change shape." Sun realized that the snake he had saved was the Dragon Prince.

Chinese Myth

The Dragon King understood that Sun was a great healer, because his son had been very badly wounded by the time the shepherd stopped beating him. So instead of rewarding Sun with money or gold, the king commanded his servants to bring a still more precious gift to the palace. Sun could not wait to see what it was and was overjoyed when the king presented him with no fewer than thirty books describing healing medicines that were known only to the dragon people.

Sun read the thirty volumes carefully, and was soon using the healing plants they described to cure all kinds of illnesses.

Right: Yao Wang (yow wang) was a legendary physician of the Tang Dynasty (618–907 C.E.) who became an immortal. This statue shows him embraced by a dragon, a symbol of good fortune.

THE ENERGY OF LIFE

China is famous for its traditional medicine, a system of healing that has existed for thousands of years. It uses all kinds of herbs that grow in the Chinese countryside, as well as the techniques of acupuncture. According to traditional Chinese medicine, a life-giving energy, called *qi* (chi), flows along a series of twelve lines, known as meridians, that run up and down the body. When something blocks the flow of *qi*, the body's natural balance is upset and illness results. It is the physician's job to get the *qi* flowing again.

One method of unblocking the flow of the *qi* is to use acupuncture, which involves inserting special needles into the body, at particular points along the meridians. Modern science has not so far found a way to explain why acupuncture works, but someone who has been properly trained can produce some impressive results, often improving the symptoms that a patient feels.

Right: A Chinese medical chart shows the path followed by a meridian and the points where needles could be inserted.

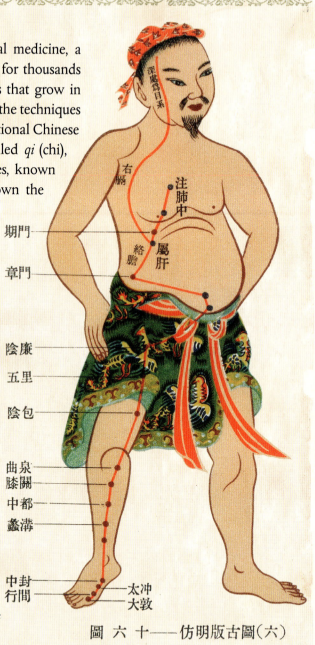

圖 六 十——仿明版古圖（六）

But he also carried on exploring the countryside, tasting all kinds of plants and testing their medicinal powers on himself before prescribing them to patients.

Sun discovered many remarkable qualities of plants, realizing that some poisonous plants became good to eat when combined and cooked with other species. People even said that parts of Sun's body were transparent, so that he could look inside and see the effects that different medicines had on his inner organs.

Sun was in great demand as a doctor, and when he finally died people were heartbroken that such a talented healer should have passed away. Everyone who knew him was determined that he should have a magnificent funeral and that he should always be remembered as one of China's greatest ever physicians. But when they went to put his body in its coffin, something extraordinary happened. Only Sun's robes were there. His body had completely disappeared. The healer had gone to heaven to take his place among the gods.

Left: Chinese physicians use many herbal remedies made from the dried leaves, stems, and roots of plants, all specially mixed to suit the patient and their specific illness.

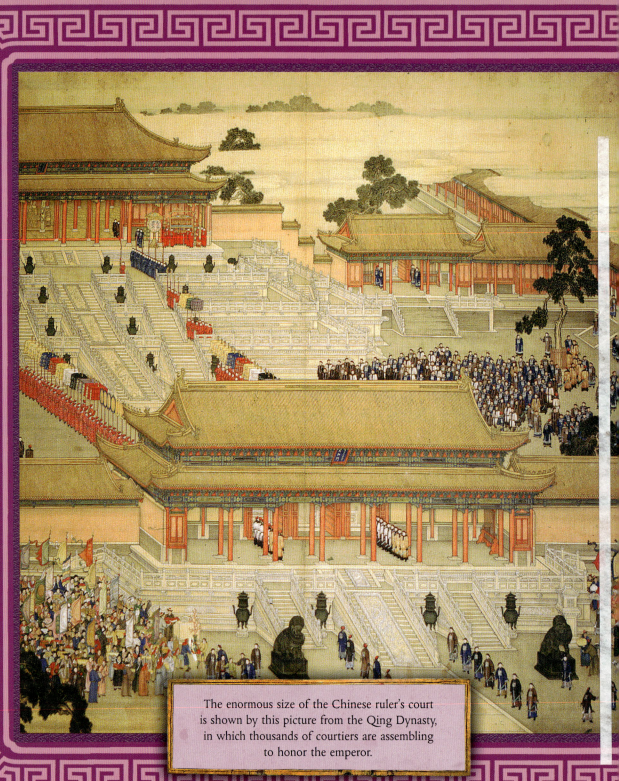

The enormous size of the Chinese ruler's court
is shown by this picture from the Qing Dynasty,
in which thousands of courtiers are assembling
to honor the emperor.

THE HEAVENLY EMPIRE

For thousands of years, China was ruled by a series of supremely powerful emperors. The first emperor was Qin Shi Huang Di, who came to power in 221 B.C.E. and was the first man to rule the whole of China as a single country. The last emperor was the boy-emperor Puyi, who was forced to step down in 1912. In order to govern this huge country, the emperors relied upon an enormous staff. This civil service was chosen by merit and was powerful and highly respected. The gods and goddesses of Chinese mythology were organized in a similar way. The supreme god, known as the Jade Emperor, Supreme Ruler, or Emperor of Heaven, had a vast staff, a kind of heavenly civil service, who helped him rule and acted as messengers between the human world and the world of the gods.

The Jade Emperor and his court were immortals who lived forever. But many of them started out as ordinary men or women. By doing some good deed or displaying some exceptional ability, they found favor with the Jade Emperor and were admitted to the ranks of the gods. The myths connected with many of these characters, such as the famous Ba Xian (pa hsi-en), or Eight Immortals, are the tales of how they left the mortal world behind to join the court of the Jade Emperor.

THE JADE EMPEROR'S COURT

The ruler of the gods was known as Yu Huang (yoo hwang), the Jade Emperor, although people also called him the Emperor of Heaven or simply the Supreme Ruler. The Jade Emperor was surrounded by hundreds of servants. These immortals influenced events on earth in all kinds of ways, from controlling the weather to helping people with their problems.

Yu Huang was such an exalted figure that few people had a clue about how he became Emperor of Heaven in the first place. But according to one story, he got his high-ranking position through cunning. Thousands of years ago, there was a war between two powerful ruling families in China, the Zhou (choo) and the Shang. The Shang king, Zhou Xin (choo hsin) and his wicked mistress were an evil pair who were cruel to their subjects, so the Chinese people were pleased when, after a series of battles, King Wu of the Zhou Dynasty, ably assisted by his prime minister and general Jiang Ziya (chang tzoo-yah), was the winner.

After his victory, King Wu gave Jiang Ziya the job of rewarding all of those from both sides who had fought bravely—and the bravest of all were to become immortals in heaven. Jiang Ziya made the most courageous war leaders gods, but kept the post of Emperor of Heaven vacant. When Jiang had finished, Wu announced that Jiang himself should become Jade Emperor. Jiang paused modestly, as if deciding whether to accept the post.

At this point, Zhang (chang), a cunning commander who had not been offered immortality, stepped forward and knelt in front of Jiang and Wu, thanking them for making him emperor! The pair were so astonished that they did not know what to say. And so it was that Zhang became Yu Huang, Jade Emperor, instead of Jiang. Poor Jiang had to be content with the job of the Jade Emperor's chief minister.

THE EMPEROR RULES JUSTLY

In spite of this difficult start, the Jade Emperor soon showed himself to be a just ruler of heaven. One of his most important tasks was to keep a record of how every human being on earth behaved during their life. To do this, he relied on reports from the household gods—often called the Kitchen Gods—who kept watch on humans all year round. Every year, toward the end of the last lunar month, the kitchen gods came to the court of the Jade Emperor and described each person's conduct. What the kitchen gods said was added to the record, along with any comments made by the Jade Emperor himself. When a person died, the records of their conduct were used to determine whether they would be reborn as a human or an animal.

The Jade Emperor was far too glorious a figure to deal directly with humans, so people did not normally try to influence him by making offerings to him at the temple. Instead they worshipped his servants and courtiers, in the hope that these lesser deities would put in a word to the Emperor on their behalf.

Left: One version of the myth of the heavenly court describes how a trio of gods hold power. At the top was the Jade Emperor himself. Beneath him were Dao Zhun (dow choon; on the right), keeper of the sacred books and ruler of the second heaven, and Laozi (on the left), founder of Daoism, royal teacher, and ruler of the third heaven.

THE GIFTS OF QUEEN XI WANGMU

After the Jade Emperor himself, the most important person at the heavenly court was Queen Xi Wangmu, also known as Jin Mu ("Golden Mother") or the Queen Mother of the West. Xi Wangmu was the wife of the Jade Emperor. She had her own residence on Mount Kunlun, where she lived surrounded by other immortals. She had the power to grant immortal life, which she could give to people by offering them one of the peaches of immortality or by prescribing a special elixir that made you immortal if you drank it.

When the archer Yi had shot down the nine suns and saved the world from drought (see pp. 22–27), he made one immortal angry. This was Di Jun, who was the father of the ten suns and wanted Yi just to frighten them into obedience, not to kill them. In revenge Di Jun forced Yi to live on earth as a mere mortal. So Yi went to ask Xi Wangmu if she could restore his immortality. The queen gave him a bottle containing the elixir, but warned him that, if he took it all, he would leave earth forever and live only with the immortals in heaven.

Yi did not want to leave earth behind, so he put off taking the elixir. But his

Right: Xi Wangmu was said to bring long life to those who worshipped her, and in this illustration carries one of the peaches of immortality in her left hand.

THE FORBIDDEN CITY

From the fifteenth to the early twentieth century C.E., the Chinese emperors lived in a huge palace complex, like a city within the city, in the center of Beijing. Only the royal family and people on the emperor's staff were allowed inside, so the complex became known as the Forbidden City. Inside the walls were luxurious living quarters for the emperor and the court, offices for royal officials, and large ceremonial halls where the emperor received visitors. All these buildings were set in beautiful gardens, crossed by streams.

Below: The Forbidden City was sealed off by high walls and a moat. Only the royal family and high-ranking civil servants could enter.

wife, who was called Chang E, liked the idea of eternal life, even though she did not want to go to heaven either.

Chang E went to see an astrologer who said that if she achieved eternal life she could go to live on the moon—away from the troubles of earth but also well away from heaven, too. So Chang E swallowed all the elixir Xi Wangmu had given Yi and set off for the moon. Sadly, she was miserable and lonely there because the only other living beings on the moon were an old man and a hare. Chang E learned the hard way that the gift of Xi Wangmu can be dangerous as well as powerful.

Confucianism

The great philosopher Kong Zi (kong zee) (551–479 B.C.E.) is better known in the West by the name Confucius. He was born at a time of social unrest, when different ruling families were fighting for control of China. Confucius traveled widely, trying to persuade people to change the way they lived to make society more stable. But few people listened to Confucius' teachings, and only much later, during the Eastern Han Dynasty (25–220 C.E.), did his ideas become popular.

Above: This portrait of Confucius shows him as a teacher, explaining his values of respect and harmony.

CONFUCIUS

The philosopher put family values at the heart of everything. He believed that children should obey their parents, and that parents should love and care for their children. There should be a similar balance in other human relationships, too: a government minister should show the same respect to his emperor, in return for his protection. If people respected each other in this way, there would be no disputes and wars.

Right: One of Confucius' great followers was Mengzi (meng-zee) (372–c. 289 B.C.E.), better known in the West as Mencius. He believed that everyone was basically good, and that their goodness could be brought out by education and work.

Right: At places like this Confucian temple in Nanjing, people come to make offerings to the gods.

TEMPLES AND RITUAL

Worship of the ancient gods and following of rituals were very important to Confucius, because he believed that, if you concentrated on rituals, you were more likely to lead a good and peaceful life. Confucian temples were full of harmonious music and the sweet smell of incense.

THE NATURAL WORLD

Although Confucius' ideas were very practical, aiming to help China toward peace, security, and better government, the philosopher also saw the importance of looking at the world of nature. As well as writing books about ritual, Confucius also taught using poetry, some of which comments on the beauty and harmony to be found in nature.

Right: The emperor Huizong painted this picture of a parakeet in the early twelfth century C.E. in a traditional Chinese style. The emperor was a poet, calligrapher, art collector, and a talented artist in his own right.

THE EIGHT IMMORTALS

The great Ba Xian, or Eight Immortals, could fly through the air, slay demons, and had the ability to remove evil from the world. But they had not always been immortal. They had once lived on earth as ordinary mortals before becoming gods as the result of their devotion to the Daoist religion.

The first of the Eight Immortals to achieve immortality was Li Xuan (lee hsoo-an), an avid student of Daoism who was taught the secret of eternal life by Xi Wangmu, the Queen Mother of the West. Li Xuan had a diseased right leg. The Queen Mother cured the disease, but Li was left lame, so she gave him an iron crutch to help him to walk.

One day Li Xuan wanted to cross a river and stepped on a floating leaf so that it could carry him across the water. When he encouraged a bystander to cross in the same way, the man refused, saying that he would sink. Li Xuan said that mortal men's cares were too heavy and the leaf would not support them. An immortal, on the other hand, had few cares, and so was as light as the air. This was why immortals could fly. Then Li Xuan stepped on the leaf once more, and floated away in the direction of the Eastern Paradise.

ZHONGLI QUAN

Zhongli Quan (chong-lee koo-an) spent his life as an officer at the emperor's court. When he was an old man, he retired from his job and traveled to the mountains to live there as a hermit. People said that he had the power to turn copper into the much more valuable metal silver. But he did not seek to make a profit from his ability. Instead he gave any money he made to the poor. On his travels he met the immortal Li Xuan, who taught him about Daoism. When he became immortal, Zhongli became the messenger of the gods.

Left: The Eight Immortals journey across the sea together. While seven crowd into the boat, Zhang Guolao rides his magical donkey. On one occasion the immortals went to a party and got drunk. They thought that it would be dangerous to fly home in such a condition, and decided that instead they would travel by sea.

SAILING

The ancient Chinese used their rivers to get around their enormous country, as sailing was easier and quicker than building roads through the rough terrain. The Chinese became skilled sailors, using their boats to make long river journeys, for fishing, and to set up ferry services across the larger rivers such as the Yangtze. They also explored the seas, using large, sturdy ships known as junks. The great age of Chinese exploration was the fifteenth century C.E., when China's sailors explored the South China Sea, the Indian Ocean, and the Arabian Sea, visiting the coasts of India and Sri Lanka and even traveling as far as the east coast of Africa. They did not attempt to conquer the lands they visited, but offered local rulers gifts, in order to set up diplomatic and trading relations.

Below: A junk is a ship with a high stern, a flat bottom, and sails stiffened with slender battens of wood.

LU DONGBIN

One day a man called Lu Dongbin arrived at an inn tired and thirsty after a long journey. Zhongli was already at the inn and was heating some rice wine. As he watched Zhongli perform this task, Lu, exhausted from his traveling, fell asleep. He dreamed that he was promoted to an important job at court and was successful for fifty years, building up a great fortune. But then he dreamed that his luck ran out and he was sent into exile. Lu woke up to see that Zhongli was still warming the rice wine—he had only been asleep for a few minutes. Lu's dream had shown him that worldly success could end in pain, so he decided to study Daoism and eventually discovered the secret of immortality.

MUSIC

Confucius believed that music was as important to human beings as food. He thought that, if people regularly sang, played an instrument, or listened to music, the harmony of the notes would enhance their own inner harmony, and therefore promote the health of both mind and body. He especially valued gentle, delicate music, fearing that loud or discordant sounds would make people behave violently or be unhappy.

Music was frequently performed in ancient China. Emperors liked to have music playing for them while they held banquets, and many people liked to listen when a storyteller set his tales to music. There were many instruments, including pipes, lutes, and a stringed instrument called a zither.

Above: This tenth-century C.E. illustration shows a woman playing reed pipes, which were among the most popular instruments.

HAN XIANGZI

Han Xiangzi (han hsi-ang-zee) was an eager student of Daoism, following in the footsteps of his great-uncle, Han Yu, who was a famous philosopher of the Tang Dynasty. Han Yu taught his great-nephew about the Daoist faith, and the young man soon knew more than his teacher, even learning how to predict the future—he foretold that Han Yu, who had fallen out with the emperor, would soon return to favor.

Realizing that Han Yu had taught him all he could, Han Xiangzi sought another master, and became a follower of the immortal Lu Dongbin. It soon became clear that Han was so wise that he was close to becoming immortal too, so Lu took him to climb the tree where the peaches of immortality grew.

When Han had almost reached the top of the tree, he missed his footing and fell, but he had climbed high enough—just before he hit the ground, he achieved immortality. Han went to live with Lu and the other immortals in the Eastern Paradise.

CAO GUOJIU

Unlike Lu Dongbin, who dreamed that he got an important job, Cao Guojiu (cow kwo-jew) really did have a high position at court: he was the brother of an empress during the Song Dynasty.

But his high position did not keep Cao Guojiu out of trouble. He was accused of being involved in a murder conspiracy and found himself in prison. After some years, Cao was released from captivity. But having learned about the short-lived and precarious nature of human power, he no longer wanted to return to court. Cao traveled into the mountains, gave away his wealth, and began life as a hermit.

But Cao kept one souvenir of his former life: the small gold tablet that every courtier carried. One day, Cao wanted to cross a river but had no money to pay the ferryman. So he showed the boatman his gold tablet, to show that he was a courtier and deserved a free passage. The ferryman was not impressed and told Cao not to pull rank. Cao responded by throwing the gold tablet into the river, to show that he had now really renounced his old privileged life. The ferryman, who was none other than the immortal Lu Dongbin, was so impressed that he taught Cao the way of Daoism. Cao later joined the ranks of the immortals.

Opposite: This painting on wood shows the immortal Cao Guojiu (standing) in his refuge among the mountains.

MAGIC

The magical powers of the Eight Immortals seem incredible today, but in ancient China many people believed in magic. Magicians played an important part in daily life and, during the Qin and Han dynasties (221 B.C.E.–220 C.E.), the emperors even employed a number of magicians.

Called *fangshi*, these men worked as healers and had the reputation of being able to make people live longer—and to make them immortal when they died. Although many people believed in their powers, the Confucian scholars who became increasingly powerful at court during the Han Dynasty were more sceptical, and the fashion for employing *fangshi* had declined by the time the Han Dynasty came to an end.

ZHANG GUOLAO

Zhang Guolao (chang kwo-low) was a hermit who possessed magical powers. The emperor and empress often tried to persuade him to come to court, but Zhang refused, preferring his quiet country life.

After many requests, Zhang finally gave in and traveled to the capital, but suddenly dropped dead by the gate of one of the temples. Miraculously, he came back to life, even though his body had started to decay, and he impressed the emperor with all kinds of powers: he could make himself invisible, drink poison without getting ill, and turn birds to stone simply by pointing at them.

Eventually Zhang returned to his home in the mountains, now an old man. When he died he was buried in a tomb near his home. Later, some of his followers opened the tomb and found it empty—for Zhang Guolao had become an immortal. He was said to ride a magical donkey or mule, which he could fold up like a sheet of paper and stow away in a bag when he did not need to travel.

Along with Lu Dongbin and Li Xuan, Zhang Guolao was an especially powerful immortal. The three were well known for their flamboyant dress and their dashing adventures fighting demons. They were sometimes so boisterous that they got themselves into trouble, by getting drunk or playing dangerous tricks such as setting fire to the ocean.

LAN CAIHE

Lan Caihe (lan tsigh-ho) was the most mysterious of the Eight Immortals, because no one was certain whether he was a man or a woman—although people usually referred to him as a man. Lan Caihe was famous as a healer and knew the medicinal powers of many herbs that grew in the Chinese countryside. Once he was walking in the mountains gathering herbs when he met an old beggar who was obviously in pain. When Lan looked under the man's rags he saw that his body was covered with sores and wounds. Quickly Lan began to wash and dress the wounds and, although this was a daunting task, he did not give up until all the beggar's boils were soothed. The sick man turned out to be the immortal Cao Guojiu, and Cao was so impressed both with Lan's healing powers and with his determination that he took him to the Eastern Paradise to become an immortal.

HE XIANGU

He Xiangu (ho hsien-koo) was a young girl who lived near a mountain range called the Mother of Pearl Mountains. One night she had a dream in which a spirit told her to go to the mountains, take some of the mother of pearl that was found there, and grind it into a powder. She should then eat the powder, and when she did so she would become immortal. When she awoke the next morning, He went to the mountain and ate the stone. And she soon joined the other immortals in the Eastern Paradise.

Right: He Xiangu was the female member of the group of Eight Immortals and was much worshipped by women.

Daoism

The philosophy of Daoism was popularized by the sage and writer Laozi, who lived in the fifth century B.C.E. Daoism, also known as Taoism, is a philosophy that stresses that all living things are linked. Whereas Confucianism focuses on the family or the state, Daoism focuses on the individual, and Daoists aim to reach a form of spiritual perfection that leads to everlasting life after death.

Above: Daoist temples contain altars where images of the immortals are placed. This temple is in Shanghai.

Below: Making offerings and burning incense are two of the rituals that take place in Daoist temples. These worshippers in Hong Kong are burning incense. Devotees hope that the smoke will carry their messages to the immortals.

THE DAOIST WAY

To achieve everlasting life, Daoists follow the *dao*, or way, which entails trying to live a simple life in harmony with nature. To begin with, Daoism was a philosophy, a way of helping people to lead a better life. But in the centuries after the death of Laozi it changed. Followers were inspired by stories of people who had become immortals from following Daoist teachings, and they began to worship these immortals as gods and goddesses. In this way Daoism became a religion with its own deities and temples.

Above: This eighteenth-century C.E. painting shows Laozi (left) meeting Confucius, who is holding the Buddha. The three men could not have met because the Buddha lived in India—portraying the three together is simply a way of showing that they were the three most important religious leaders to influence China.

LAOZI

Laozi worked as an archivist in the emperor's palace, but after a while he tired of that life and left to lead the life of a traveling sage. When someone he met asked him about his ideas, he wrote a book called *Dao De Jing* (tow tay ching; "The Way and Its Power"). The *Dao De Jing* is still the most important Daoist text.

YIN AND YANG

According to Daoism, everything in the world is made up of two basic elements, called *yin* and *yang*. In nature, these two elements are held in a delicate balance. When things go wrong—when someone is ill, there is a war, or a river floods—it is because of an imbalance in yin and yang. The traditional way to represent yin and yang is as a circle divided into a light and a dark section by an S-shaped line, representing the way the two elements flow into each other.

Below: In this plate from a Daoist temple, the Yin and Yang symbols are surrounded by the eight trigrams (see pp. 34–35).

SAFE AS HOUSES

The god Zao Jun (tsow chun) is often known as the Kitchen God, or the God of the Stove. Chinese people sometimes put up his portrait in the kitchen, above the stove. But he was not always a powerful god: he was once an ill-fated mortal man named Chang.

When Chang was a young man, he married a girl called Guoding Xiang (kwo-ting hsian). Guoding was everything a man could want in a wife: gentle, attractive, faithful, and a good cook! With his young wife's help, Chang soon began to do well in business and became quite rich.

AN UNLUCKY MARRIAGE

But the couple's happiness did not last long. Another woman, Li Hai Tang, decided she wanted to marry Chang, and soon she had persuaded him to divorce Guoding and marry her. But without Guoding at his side, Chang did not do so well in business and his money gradually dwindled away. When he became poor, the faithless Li lost interest in Chang, and soon she left him.

Chang was on his own, poor, and miserable. He took to wandering the streets as a beggar. Lack of food and shelter made him ill and, after a few years, he began to lose his eyesight. One day Chang was wandering around begging as usual when he happened to pass the house of his first wife.

When Guoding spotted Chang she recognized him immediately, even though he was dressed in rags and looked much older than when they had been married. She took pity on him, invited him in, and cooked him a dish of noodles. Chang did not realize who this kind woman was as he was now completely blind. He ate the noodles ravenously and told Guoding that they tasted delicious, just as good as the noodles his first wife used to make.

When Guoding saw how appreciative Chang was, she said, "Chang, open your eyes!" And straight away Chang's sight was miraculously restored.

Left: The Kitchen God Zao Jun is usually portrayed as a bearded man in the robes of a scholar. In this illustration he is accompanied by a band of musicians playing traditional instruments.

Of course the first thing Chang saw was his former wife. But instead of being pleased he was full of shame for the way he had treated her. Overcome by remorse, he jumped straight into the fire. Guoding grabbed hold of his leg to try to pull him out of the flames, but he was too determined. Chang was swiftly consumed by the flames, leaving Guoding in tears, grasping the leg that had come away from his burning body.

CHANG GAINS IMMORTALITY

Because of his genuine remorse, Chang was allowed to join the immortals after his sad death. He became an important god, known as Zao Jun. It is not surprising that he became the God of the Stove. And because the stove, used for both heating and cooking, is the heart of a traditional Chinese house, Zao Jun was soon one of the best loved of the gods.

People said that Zao Jun was especially offended by swearing and bad language. Everyone was expected to be respectful to his image and to behave well, especially in the kitchen itself. He did not like wasted food and was offended if people made a promise—for example to live without eating meat for a period of time—and then broke their vow.

Although he was not a member of the Jade Emperor's court, Zao Jun had a very important job. He acted as a messenger between earth and heaven and it was his role to report on the behavior of humanity, so the Jade Emperor had a full record of what went on on earth. People believed that when something was burned, the smoke rose to the sky and took a message to heaven. So at every New Year the paper image of Zao Jun was taken down from above the stove and burned, sending a report to the Jade Emperor about the family's behavior during the previous year.

The ceremony of burning the image of the Kitchen God was one of the most important in the religious year, so people prepared for it very carefully. The usual custom was to make an offering of some of the most tempting sweets a few days before New Year. The householder left these on the stove, by the god's image. Then the image itself, which could get rather sooty from the smoke from the fire, was cleaned. Sometimes some sugar or wine was smeared on the god's face, to help persuade Zao Jun to give a good report when he arrived in heaven. Finally, the image was taken down and burned, and the higher the smoke rose the happier people were, because they believed his report was reaching heaven. A new image was put up in the kitchen shortly afterward.

CHINESE HOUSES

Traditional Chinese houses were often quite large because each one was usually home to several generations of the same family. Homes were built around one or more courtyards, with the main courtyard acting as a meeting place for family members. Like a small garden, it often had a tree in the middle and there were usually pots containing flowers.

At the far end, away from the street, was either the main building, where the most senior members of the household lived, or the entrance to an inner courtyard, again for the older family members. To either side of the courtyard were buildings where relatives lived or where guests stayed. The kitchens were built conveniently near the main building, and if the family was rich enough to have servants, their rooms would be near the kitchens. Many traditional houses like this still survive, although many were replaced by modern-style homes during the twentieth century.

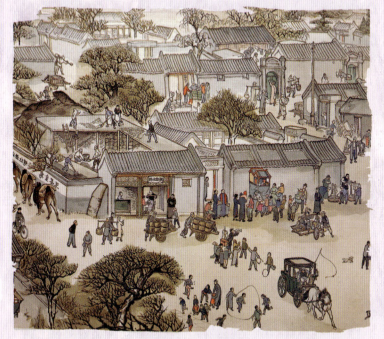

Left: Traditional courtyard homes can be seen in this painting of summertime in Beijing at the start of the twentieth century.

Statues of the Buddha, usually showing him in a pose of quiet contemplation, became common as the faith spread across China. This one is in Jingshan Park in Beijing.

MYTHS OF BUDDHISM

The Buddhist faith has proved a rich source of Chinese myths. As well as the Buddha himself, Chinese Buddhism features many other religious leaders and teachers who show people how to lead a better life, in the hope that they will eventually reach a state of fulfillment or enlightenment.

There are many myths involving these characters, but Chinese Buddhist myth does not exist in isolation. Characters from traditions outside Buddhism can enter Buddhist myth, meet the Buddha, and learn important lessons about life. It is not unusual for a single mythical story to include characters from the Daoist religion, the Buddha, and figures from the ranks of the traditional gods and goddesses of China. Like the vast land of China itself, Chinese myths contain influences from far and wide, and in some of the longest and most famous stories, like the tale of Monkey, all these different elements come together.

IN THE
WESTERN PARADISE

Of all the Buddhist deities, the most powerful was Amituo Fu, the gentle buddha, or "enlightened person," who promised everlasting life to those who had faith in him. He began life as a mortal long ago in India, where he was named Dharmakara. When he was a young man, he was inspired by the simple life led by the Buddha, who had renounced comfort and riches in order to find out how to reach a higher state of fulfillment, known as enlightenment.

Dharmakara decided to become a Buddhist monk and, under the guidance of a wise teacher, meditated for many long years, steadily coming closer and closer to enlightenment.

Gradually Dharmakara decided that his own vision of fulfillment was rather different from the usual goal of personal enlightenment. He did not simply want enlightenment for himself, but wanted to bring others to enlightenment as well. After considerable thought, he made a promise.

Dharmakara announced that he would not become a buddha himself unless he could save all living things and set up a heavenly kingdom where they would all be able to enjoy everlasting life. This amazing vow brought the monk so much merit that he did indeed become a buddha himself, after which time he was known in India as Amitabha, and in China as Amituo Fu.

Amituo Fu went to live in a heavenly kingdom in the west, one of four Buddhist kingdoms at the four points of the compass, known as the Western Paradise or sometimes as the Pure Land. This was an ideal land where everything was beautiful. There were no fires or darkness, no violence or suffering, but everything, from the gardens to the palaces, was arranged to make those who dwelled there contented and at peace.

PAGODAS

A pagoda is a tall tower on which each story has its own overhanging roof. Pagodas are among the most beautiful structures in Asian architecture, elegantly designed and often displaying many statues of the Buddha. Pagodas were first built at Buddhist shrines in India and spread to China when Buddhism took hold there. They came in various different shapes and sizes. They could be octagonal, hexagonal, or square, and had different numbers of floors, although they were always tall.

Pagodas began as monuments built over the burial-place of the ashes of a particularly saintly Buddhist monk. The structures became popular in China during the Tang Dynasty (618–906 C.E.), and in the centuries that followed it was normal for every Chinese Buddhist monastery to have at least one pagoda.

Right: Numerous pagodas survive in China today. Like many others, this pagoda in the Red and Gold Temple in Hong Kong is eight-sided.

THE PURE LAND

The Western Paradise was a place of amazing natural wonders. The many trees included banana trees full of ripe fruit and jewel trees made of gems and precious metals such as gold and silver, emeralds and pearls.

Enormous lotus flowers—some of them several miles across—bloomed all year round. Countless rays extended from these lotus flowers, and at the end of each ray sat a buddha, looking down on the world with calm and compassion. Every buddha was surrounded by a halo of light, purity, and peace, so all these buddhas, with their adjoining haloes, made the Western Paradise the most perfect place imaginable.

The rivers of the Western Paradise flowed slowly and steadily, and beautiful scents rose up from their waters to delight the passerby. As the waters ran by they made all kinds of beautiful sounds, which combined together made the most melodious music one could ever hear, gentle and moving to the heart, and endlessly changing so that no listener would ever tire of hearing it. If someone wanted to bathe in the rivers, their waters could be as hot or cold as they wished them to be.

Listening to these lovely sounds and looking at the gorgeous trees and flowers was so pleasing and so calming that anyone in the Western Paradise was soon brought to a state of peace and compassion. In this way, the Western Paradise itself helped people toward the state of enlightenment that they wished to gain by practicing Buddhism on earth.

Amituo Fu said that all would be able to come to the Western Paradise who had faith in him, who did not commit certain serious crimes or sins, and who did not speak disparagingly of the true religion of Buddhism. Many people believed that, if they sincerely announced their faith in Amituo Fu, they would be admitted to Paradise. As a result, devotion to Amituo Fu became popular all over China.

Right: This image of Amituo Fu in the Western Paradise comes from a cave temple at Dunhuang (doon-hwang), a Chinese town at the edge of the Gobi Desert, which contains some of the most beautiful Buddhist paintings in the world.

Ever since Amituo Fu became a buddha, people in China have offered prayers to him. Many people pray to him both in times of difficulty, when it is hoped that the gentle buddha will make things better, and in times of happiness, when people want to thank the buddha for everything that he has done for them.

His name is also often included on tombstones, especially of those who have died young, so that anyone who reads the inscription will automatically utter a prayer to Amituo Fu, thereby helping the soul of the dead person on their way to the Paradise in the West.

Buddhism in China

The Buddhist faith began in India during the sixth century B.C.E. and was based on the teachings of Siddhartha Gautama (c. 563–483 B.C.E.), known as the Buddha ("the enlightened one"). Buddhism did not arrive in China until long afterward, probably around the time of the collapse of the Han Dynasty in 220 C.E. After Han rule ended, China was ruled by people from Central Asia who brought Buddhist monks with them as civil servants. Buddhism spread quickly through China, where it developed features that were distinctly different from Buddhism in India.

Left: The founder of Buddhism, the Buddha is revered as a teacher. Gigantic statues of him, like this one cut out of a rocky hillside at Leshan, were erected in many places in China.

Above: *Bodhisattvas* are often portrayed in pictures and carvings, such as these at the Longmen Caves in Hunan province, China. Construction of the caves began in 493 C.E.

THE BUDDHA

Siddhartha Gautama was an Indian prince who gave up a life of luxury to seek higher truths. He taught that, by following a way of life involving wisdom, good behavior, and meditation, people could be led away from the suffering of the world to reach an ideal state called nirvana or enlightenment.

Left: Mountains tower toward the heavens and are remote places of great grandeur and beauty. It is not surprising that many Chinese mountains, like this one, Hua Shan (hwa shan), are seen as holy places. Many have links with specific *bodhisattvas*, and there are temples on their slopes that are regularly visited by pilgrims.

Below: These Buddhist monks, in their traditional robes, have gathered for a religious festival in Qinghai province in western China.

BODHISATTVAS

A key difference between Chinese Buddhism and the kind practiced in India is that many Chinese Buddhists believe that, if they have faith in the compassionate buddha Amituo Fu, they can live on after death in the Western Paradise or Pure Land. Followers of this form of Buddhism are known as Pure Land Buddhists. They believe that the best way to show your faith is to become a *bodhisattva*, a buddha or enlightened person, who reaches the point of nirvana, but turns back, in order to help others achieve the enlightened state.

MONASTERIES

Monasteries play a major role in Buddhist life, especially in the Buddhism of Tibet and western China. As well as providing ideal places for a life of contemplation, they are also beneficial to the rest of the population, who achieve "merit," and therefore move closer to enlightenment, by donating food to the monks.

THE MERCIFUL GODDESS

The goddess Guan Yin began life as the princess Miao Shan (meeow shan), the daughter of a Chinese emperor of the Chou Dynasty. Miao Shan's father wanted her to marry a wealthy prince, to increase the prestige of the imperial family. But Miao Shan did not want to get married—her ambition was to enter a nunnery.

Miao Shan's father tried to persuade her to do what she was told and get married, but the girl insisted. She was absolutely certain that she wanted to devote her life to religion. In the end, the emperor said that she could join a nunnery—but he had a cunning plan.

The emperor had a long conversation with the abbess of a nunnery, explaining that his daughter was so devoted to her duty that she should do all the worst jobs: menial tasks like cleaning and heavy work like carrying big loads. Secretly he hoped that Miao Shan would be put off the nunnery for good, and beg to return to the palace and get married.

Yet the emperor's plans did not work out. Miao Shan put up with her degrading duties with cheerfulness, and it became clear that she did not want to leave the nunnery at all. The girl's determination overwhelmed the emperor with anger. How could his young daughter disobey him like this! Wild with fury, he ordered that his daughter be executed.

AN EXECUTION

Miao Shan was brought to the place of execution and a swordsman brought down his razor-sharp sword on her neck. But a miraculous thing happened—as it fell, the weapon shattered into a thousand pieces, leaving Miao Shan unscathed.

The enraged emperor ordered that his daughter should be strangled. His command was obeyed, and as the girl's body slumped lifeless, her soul escaped, making its way straight to the underworld.

The soul of the virtuous girl passed quickly through the underworld and soon reached paradise. When she arrived there she announced that she would rather return to earth to help the countless people who needed aid—and so Miao Shan was reborn as the merciful goddess Guan Yin, which means "hearing the cry."

HEARING THE CRY

Soon after she returned to earth, Guan Yin heard that her father was seriously ill. She knew that the only thing that would cure him was a medicine made of one of her own eyes and one of her arms.

So, setting aside her own terrible pain, she sacrificed her own body to make such a potion. She sent the elixir to her father, who was quickly cured.

The emperor was flabbergasted. He realized that he had underestimated his daughter and the power of Buddhism. Not only did he become a Buddhist but he ordered a statue to be made of his daughter, and in this statue she was depicted with one thousand arms, restoring the flesh that she had sacrificed for him a thousandfold.

Left: This porcelain statuette shows the goddess of mercy Guan Yin with an expression of calm contemplation on her face.

PAPER AND PRINTING

The Chinese were experimenting with papermaking during the Han Dynasty (207 B.C.E.–220 C.E.). By the seventh century C.E., they were beginning to develop the printing process, some 800 years before it was invented in Europe. Printers worked out how to carve writing and pictures into blocks of wood, which they then covered with ink and pressed onto sheets of paper. Although they had no complex machinery to help them, a skilled printer could produce up to 1,500 pages a day with wood blocks. It is likely that most of the early printers were Buddhists who used their skill to produce copies of the Buddhist scriptures.

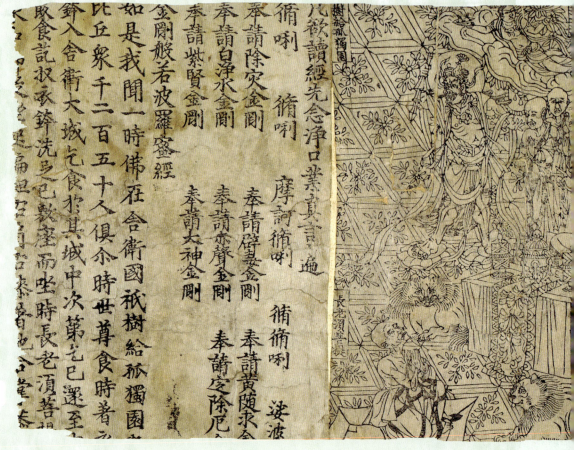

To this day, many statues of Guan Yin in Chinese temples show her with a thousand arms, or with so many that she seems to have a thousand.

Guan Yin continued to travel around the world answering people's prayers and helping the sick and needy. She became a particular friend of childless couples, helping them to have children. She loved to help families sort out their arguments and differences, so that both children and parents could see each other's points of view, just as her father had finally been able to see her point of view about her mission to help and heal.

Guan Yin's power and mercy were so great that soon everyone in difficulty appealed to her. She would help women in childbirth, comfort people with sick relatives or who had recently suffered a bereavement, and give strength to those who were about to do some challenging task such as go on a long journey or begin a new business venture.

The merciful goddess played one other vital role: she helped to comfort souls in the underworld. Daoists, who believed that souls spent time being judged in the underworld before passing on to paradise, asked her to help the souls of their departed loved ones through this ordeal, so she became as important to them as to Buddhists. And to this day, people still make offerings of tea, fruit, or money to Guan Yin, convinced that she will help all who pray to her through life's difficulties. Her statue can be seen in millions of homes and temples throughout China.

Left: The oldest Chinese printed book to survive is a Buddhist text, known as the *Diamond Sutra*, which was printed in 868 C.E. and is a 16-ft-long (5 m) scroll. A *sutra* is a manual, or collection of rules or ideas. Buddhists still read the *Diamond Sutra*, which summarizes a number of key ideas of the form of Buddhism popular in China, Mongolia, and other Far Eastern countries.

MONKEY

Soon after he was born in the forest, Monkey became a brilliant magician. To improve his skills further, he studied with a Daoist immortal, who taught him all kinds of magic. Monkey learned how to leap thousands of miles through the air and how to change his shape whenever he wanted to. He was easily the most skilled and powerful member of his species to walk the earth.

Monkey's skills were second to none, but he could not resist playing tricks on people and he often got into trouble. Eventually the Daoists with whom he was studying threw him out and Monkey returned to his fellow animals in the forest. Soon he became leader of all the other monkeys, using his magic powers to conquer their enemies.

All the apes and monkeys of the forest were so impressed with Monkey's skills that they held a great feast in his honor. But the celebration got out of hand. Monkey drank too much and fell into a drunken stupor. While he was asleep the king of the underworld arrived and captured Monkey, and soon the hapless animal found himself chained up in the dungeons of hell.

PUNISHING MONKEY

But Monkey's powers enabled him to escape. He broke his chains and, before anyone had realized it, stole the register of judgments. This was the book in which the judges of the underworld wrote down the details of everyone's life and death. Monkey turned to his own page and found that he was listed as dying at the age of 342. This was not old enough for Monkey, so he crossed out his name and age from the book—as well as those of many of his monkey family, too. From this point, he was destined to become an immortal.

The judges of the underworld decided that they should go to the Jade Emperor himself to complain about Monkey's antics and to ask him to come up with a suitable punishment. When the emperor got to hear of what Monkey had done he was angry. His first instinct

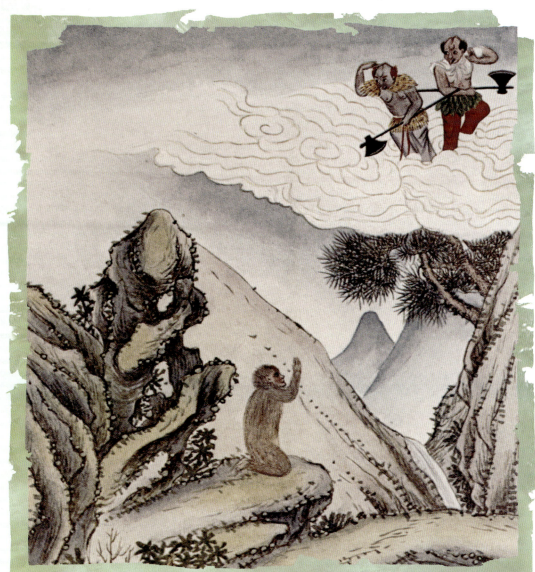

Above: Immortals look down from heaven on the young Monkey in this early twentieth-century C.E. painting. The trickster is already waving a paw boldly at the onlookers.

was to summon a vast army to deal with the animal. But he changed his mind. Rather than waste the efforts of his soldiers, he decided that the best way to treat the trickster was to give him a job to keep him busy. So Monkey was made overseer of the Emperor's stables and for a while he was well behaved.

To begin with, Monkey thought that his grand-sounding job was an important position. But he soon realized that it was not a very powerful post, and that the emperor had given him the job to keep him out of trouble. So he grew restless and began his mischief once more. This time, he became a vandal, going around breaking up the Jade Emperor's palace and causing all kinds of problems. When the Jade Emperor sent soldiers to stop him, Monkey ran away up Mount Huaguo (hwa-gwo), and whatever the emperor's troops did to try to bring him down, Monkey stopped them by using his magic powers.

After this had gone on for a while, the Jade Emperor saw that the best thing would be to come to an agreement with Monkey. So once more, the emperor gave the mischief-maker a job, this time looking after the heavenly peach garden, where the trees bearing the peaches of immortality grew. Eating these marvelous fruits made you live forever.

THE HEAVENLY PEACH GARDEN

All went well until the gods held a peach festival in the garden and forgot to invite Monkey. It was an important festival, to celebrate the birthday of Xi Wangmu, the Queen Mother of the West, and the trickster was angry when he found out that he had been left off the invitation list. So before the party began, Monkey crept into the garden, gathered up all the peaches, and ate them all. He had not only spoiled the celebrations but had fulfilled his destiny—he was now one of the immortals.

Monkey then fled the garden and ran off to the home of the Daoist sage Laozi, where he caused more trouble by stealing the sage's pills of immortality. He even ate one of the pills—to make doubly sure that he really was immortal. The power of the peaches and Laozi's pills would make Monkey an even more troublesome enemy for the gods. He ran away from Laozi's home, chuckling at the mischief he would be able to do.

Before long, Monkey was making yet more trouble, attempting to take over heaven before he once again climbed Mount Huagao to hide from the soldiers of the Jade Emperor. This time the Emperor realized that things had got serious and decided Monkey should be put to death. But of course this was impossible as Monkey had eaten both the peaches and Laozi's pill of immortality. When the Emperor discovered this, he did not know what to do. He asked for the advice of the Buddha. Perhaps the great teacher would have a peaceful solution where war and punishment had failed.

Opposite: People imagined that the heavenly peach garden was a place of great beauty, where peach trees grew against a backdrop of stunning mountain scenery. This painting of the garden was the work of an artist of the Ming Dynasty (1368–1644 C.E.).

MONKEY IS SUMMONED BY BUDDHA

The Buddha called Monkey to him and started to question him. When Monkey was asked why he wanted to rule heaven, he replied that he was clever and powerful enough to do so.

"Everyone knows that I can travel thousands of miles in a single leap," he said.

The Buddha replied that, if Monkey could really achieve this, he should rule heaven, but that he doubted if Monkey could even jump out of his hand.

Monkey replied not with words but with the mightiest leap he had ever made. He traveled far, landing at the foot of a tall mountain and writing his name on one of the rocks before bounding back to report to the Buddha what he had done. But the Buddha laughed when Monkey said he had crossed the whole world in one leap. He showed the trickster the mountain where he had written his name—it was simply the base of one of the Buddha's great fingers.

Monkey refused to believe what the Buddha told him, so the teacher told Monkey to make the leap again, to check for himself. As Monkey jumped, the Buddha closed his hand, carefully imprisoning Monkey in his fist. He then handed the trickster over to the merciful goddess Guan Yin, to come up with a suitable punishment.

Guan Yin created a magic mountain and locked Monkey inside. He was told he would have to spend hundreds of years inside the mountain, and that when he truly repented of his sins he would be let out again.

After centuries had passed, the Buddha and Guan Yin decided that the time had come for Monkey to be released. The Buddha came up with a great challenge for Monkey. He was told to accompany the sage T'ang Seng (tang seng), who was going on a long pilgrimage to India to bring back Buddhist scriptures to China.

Right: Monkeys, with their amusing antics and similarity to humans, fascinated people throughout the history of China. This monkey-shaped wine container dates from the Tang Dynasty (618–906 C.E.).

THE QILIN

Chinese myths are full of animals that played a special part in the lives of humans and the gods. One of the most famous was the *qilin* (chee-lin), which was the Chinese equivalent of the Western unicorn. The *qilin* had the body of a deer, the hooves of a horse, and a single horn. Along its back were hairs of various different colors. The *qilin* was said to be a creature that worked for justice in the world. When a wise or just emperor took the throne, a *qilin* was said to appear so that people would realize that the ruler had these good qualities.

When Yongle (yong-li) (1403–1424 C.E.) became emperor, an admirer sent a giraffe to his court as a gift. Many people thought that this creature—then unknown in China—was so unusual that it must be a *qilin*. Yongle was revered as a just ruler as a result, and when he turned out to be an able ruler, people must have had their belief in the power of the *qilin* strengthened. According to one story, the creature was meant to take part in criminal trials, and if it found a person guilty, was said to skewer the prisoner on its horn.

Right: This picture of a *qilin* forms an embroidered badge which once adorned the robe of an official who worked at the court of the emperor during the sixteenth or seventeenth century C.E. The badge was probably meant to suggest that the wearer behaved with justice when he was carrying out his work.

By a huge effort of will, Monkey managed to make the entire pilgrimage without once making mischief. He only used his magical powers when he and T'ang Seng got into trouble on their long and perilous journey. On Monkey's return, the Jade Emperor and the Buddha were so impressed with him that they promoted him to the highest rank in heaven. He was made god of victorious strife, and he has been famous ever since.

Timeline of China

c. 1580 B.C.E.
The first of the Shang kings comes to the throne; they encourage the development of metalworking and the Chinese written script.

c. 604 B.C.E.
Laozi born.

551 B.C.E.
Confucius born.

403 B.C.E.
A prolonged period of conflict, known as the Warring States Period, begins; it divides China.

221 B.C.E.
Qin Shi Huang Di, the first emperor of the Qin Dynasty, unites China and begins ambitious building projects including the Great Wall and his own tomb at Mount Li.

207 B.C.E.
The emperor Gaodi (gow-dee), founds the Han Dynasty.

124 B.C.E.
A system of competitive examinations is introduced as a qualification to enter the Chinese civil service.

119 B.C.E.
The Han Dynasty nationalizes cast iron production, so that the emperor can take all the profits from the industry.

C.E. 31
Water power is used to operate bellows to produce the current of air needed in iron furnaces.

C.E. 80
"Dragon's back" pump is first described.

C.E. 105
The first evidence for the Chinese invention of paper.

C.E. 175
A project begins to produce accurate texts of the Confucian classic books and to inscribe them on around 50 stone tablets at the Imperial Academy.

C.E. 220
Buddhism is by now well established in China.

C.E. 435
The emperor Wendi (wen-dee) curbs the power of Buddhism by allowing new temples to be built only with imperial permission.

C.E. 600
Around 90 percent of the people of China are Buddhists.

C.E. 609
The Grand Canal, linking northern and southern China, is completed.

C.E. 618
The emperor Gaozu founds the Tang Dynasty, beginning a period when the arts and literature flourish.

C.E. 635
A monk called Alopen settles in the city of Changan and founds the first Christian church in China.

C.E. 653
The earliest surviving Chinese law code is drawn up.

C.E. 725
A Chinese Buddhist monk makes the world's first mechanical clock.

C.E. 751
Muslim forces defeat the Chinese at the Battle of Talas River, stopping the Chinese army from expanding beyond the Pamir Mountains in the far west of the country.

C.E. 782
Nanchan Temple, Shanxi Province, is China's earliest surviving wooden building.

C.E. 868
The *Diamond Sutra*, a Buddhist text, is printed; it is the oldest surviving printed book in the world.

C.E. 960
The emperor Taizu (tie-zoo) founds the Song Dynasty, a period in which Chinese industry prospers. The emperor introduces a Grand Council of ministers and advisers to help him rule.

C.E. 971
The *Buddhist Canon*, a large collection of Buddhist scriptures, is printed.

C.E. 1007
A shortage of copper coins leads to the decision to print the first paper money.

C.E. 1044
A formula for gunpowder is published for the first time.

1213
The Mongol leader Genghis Khan attacks the northern plains of China until the Chinese buy him off.

1215
Genghis again attacks northern China, but then decides to move westward, leaving China free from further assaults.

1279
The Mongol leader Khubilai conquers China and establishes the Yuan Dynasty, which rules China for almost 100 years.

1368
The emperor Hongwu (hong-woo) founds the Ming Dynasty and brings the country under Chinese leadership once more.

1405
The Chinese launch a series of sea expeditions lead by admiral Zheng He to Borneo, India, Africa, and the Arabian Peninsula.

1644
After the collapse of the Ming Dynasty, a foreign ruling family, the Manchus from Manchuria to the northeast of China, founds the Qing (Ching) Dynasty, which endures until 1912.

1645
The Manchus make Chinese men wear the Manchu hairstyle.

1840
Britain and China fight a war for control of the opium trade.

1842
The Opium War ends with the Treaty of Nanjing.

1905
The civil service examination system is abolished.

1911
China becomes a republic.

1912
Puyi, the last emperor of China, steps down from power.

GLOSSARY

acupuncture System of traditional Chinese medicine in which the physician treats the patient by inserting needles into certain points on the patient's body.

ba gua The Eight Trigrams, a series of eight symbols, each made up of three continuous or broken lines, used to predict what may happen in the future.

bodhisattva A Buddhist saint, or person who, having almost reached the ultimate spiritual goal of enlightenment, holds off from reaching the enlightened state in order to help others achieve the goal.

Buddha Name meaning "the Enlightened One" and applied to the founder of the Buddhist faith (the Buddha) or to one who has achieved either enlightenment or the state of a bodhisattva.

Buddhism Religious faith founded in India by Gautama Siddhartha, known as the Buddha, during the 6th century B.C.E. and which was established to China by the early-3rd century C.E.

cardinal directions The four points of the compass – North, South, East, and West.

civil service Body of paid officials who carry out the day-to-day business of a nation or empire.

Confucianism Chinese belief system founded on the teachings of the sage Kong Zi, known as Confucius.

court The group of people most closely associated with the emperor and who include his close family, advisers, and most important servants.

culture hero Mythical being who helps to found a particular culture or civilization.

Daoism (also known as Taosim) Chinese belief system based on the teachings of the immortal Loazi.

dragon Mythical creature with a scaly body, whiskery face, and horns; in China, dragons were closely associated with the emperor and were believed to be wise, strong beings who were bringers of good fortune.

dredging Clearing a river or canal by scooping up mud or rubbish from the bottom.

dynasty Chinese ruling family. Emperors are identified by the dynasty to which they belonged. Amongst the most important

dynasties were the Qin (Chin: 221–207 B.C.E.), the Han (207 B.C.E.–220 C.E.), the Tang (618–906 C.E.), the Ming (1368-1644), and the Qing (Ching: 1644–1912).

elixir A magical liquid said to have the ability to make a person live longer or to make them immortal.

enlightenment The final spiritual goal of Buddhists, a state of complete knowledge and release from suffering.

hermit Person who lives a life apart from other people in order to seek spiritual fulfillment or truth.

immortal Being who will live forever. Chinese immortals were either gods and goddesses who had always existed or those who had been born as humans but were made immortal because of their outstanding behavior or insight.

incense Substance that is burned, to produce a fragrant odor, during religious ceremonies.

Jade Emperor The ruler of heaven, the most powerful being in Chinese mythology; also known as the Supreme Being.

lunar month The time taken for the Moon to travel around the Earth.

meridian One of a number of invisible paths or channels, running through the human body, along which energy is said to travel.

Pure Land The paradise to which according to the Pure Land school of Chinese Buddhism, the souls of the faithful go after death; also known as the Western Paradise.

sedan chair Covered chair in which a person is carried by two servants, who hold the chair on long poles.

sutra A manual or collection of rules and idea, generally regarded as the teachings of the Buddha.

terracotta Hard, unglazed pottery made from brownish/reddish clay.

trigram Symbol made up of three parts; specifically the symbols making up the *ba gua* or eight trigrams.

Western Paradise *See* **Pure Land**.

yin and yang The two natural substances or forces out of which, according to ancient Chinese thought, everything was made. It was thought that any disruption of the balance between yin and yang was harmful.

FOR MORE INFORMATION

BOOKS

The following is a selection of books that have been used in the making of this volume, plus recommendations for further reading.

Birch, Cyril. *Tales from China*. Oxford: Oxford University Press, 2000.

Birrell, Anne. *Chinese Mythology: An Introduction*. Baltimore: Johns Hopkins University Press, 1993.

Christie, Anthony. *Chinese Mythology*. London: Paul Hamlyn, 1968.

Cotterell, Arthur. *China Eyewitness Guide*. London: Dorling Kinderlsey, 1994.

Duane, O. B., and Hutchinson, N. *Chinese Myths and Legends*. London: Brockhampton Press, 1998.

Ebrey, Patricia Buckley. *The Cambridge Illustrated History of China*. Cambridge: Cambridge University Press, 2003.

Paludan, Ann. *Chronicle of the Chinese Emperors*. London: Thames & Hudson, 2003.

Shaughnessy, Edward, ed. *China: The Land of the Heavenly Dragon*. London: Duncan Baird Publishers, 2000.

Stevens, Keith. *Chinese Gods*. London: Collins and Brown, 1997.

Walters, Derek. *Chinese Mythology: An Encyclopedia of Myth and Legend*. Timonium, MD: Diamond Books, 1995.

Wong, Eva. *Tales of the Taoist Immortals*. Boston: Shambhala, 2001.

WEB SITES

http://www.chinavista.com/experience/myth/myth.html
Overview of Chinese mythology, focusing on its history and special features, and the style and art of Chinese writing.

http://www.livingmyths.com/Chinese.htm
Brief information on belief systems and creation myth. Part of a web site on mythology, which includes Greek and Celtic myths.

http://www.pantheon.org/areas/mythology/asia/chinese/
Many short articles on Chinese gods and goddesses and places of importance in Chinese mythology.

http://www.chinatown-online.co.uk/pages/culture/legends/
A selection of Chinese legends and myths, including a creation myth and tales of Confucius.

SPELLING AND PRONUNCIATION

The Chinese language uses its own unique script, and there are various methods of "Romanization," the process of converting Chinese words into western letters. The method of Romanization used in this book is based on the pinyin system. This is designed to represent as accurately as possible the pronunciation of the words in Chinese, but to help make them easier to pronounce in English, the book also gives a simplified pronunciation guide in brackets where the word first appears. But there is no accurate way of writing down the sounds of the Chinese language using western letters, so these pronunciation guides are only approximate. As an additional guide, some of the rough English equivalents of the more difficult Chinese letters are given here.

ao roughly equals English **ow** as in **cow**
b roughly equals English **p** as in **spot**
c roughly equals English **ts** as in **sits**
d roughly equals English **t** as in **stop**
g roughly equals English **k** as in **skill**
q roughly equals English **ch** as in **chill**
x roughly equals English **hs**
z roughly equals English **ds** as in **bids**
zh roughly equals English **ch**

INDEX

ACKNOWLEDGMENTS

Sources: AA = Art Archive   **BAL** = Bridgeman Art Library
Scala = Scala, Florence   **AKG** = akg-images
LPC = Lord Price Collection   **WFA** = Werner Forman Archive

b = bottom c = center t = top l = left r = right

Front cover: Corbis
Back cover: top The Lord Price Collection; **bottom** Corbis

Pages: 1 Corbis/Zefa/Jose Fuste Raga; **3** Corbis/Free Agents Limited;
7 Corbis/Burstein Collection; **8** BAL/Bibliotheque Nationale, Paris;
10 Corbis/Keren Su; **13** courtesy of Nilesh Mistry/DK images/Illustrated
Dictionary of Mythology p46; **14** WFA/Metropolitan Museum of Art,
New York; **15** Corbis/Jim Zuckerman; **17** Corbis/Asian Art & Archaeology,
Inc.; **18** LPC; **20t** AA/Freer Gallery of Art; **20b** Alamy/China Span/
Keren Su; **21t** Corbis/Gavriel Jecan; **21b** WFA/Private Collection;
23 Cambridge University Library, reprinted: Shanghai, Shangwu 1934
permission of the Syndics Cambridge; **24** BAL/V&A Museum; **27** BAL/
British Museum; **29** Corbis/Liang Zhuoming; **30** Cambridge University
Library reprinted: Shanghai, Shangwu 1934 permission of the Syndics

Cambridge; **32** BAL/ Indianapolis Museum of Art; **35** AA/Private
Collection/Marc Charmet; **36–37** Corbis/Keren Su; **38** AKG; **39** Corbis/
Mike McQueen; **40c** Corbis/Pierre Colombe; **40b** AA/Freer Gallery of
Art; **41t** Corbis/Dallas & John Heaton/Free Agents Limited; **41b** AA/
Musée Guimet, Paris; **43** Corbis/Liu Liqun; **44bl** Corbis/Christie's
Images; **44br** Corbis/Burstein Collection; **47** AKG/Francois Guénet;
48 Scala Archives/British Library; **49** Science Photo Library/Mark de
Fraeye; **50** AA/Palace Museum, Beijing; **53–54** LPC; **55** Corbis/Yang
Liu; **56t** AKG; **56b** LPC; **57t** Corbis/Liu Liqun; **57b** Corbis/Burstein
Collection; **59** BAL/Private Collection; **60** Corbis/Nik Wheeler;
61 WFA/National Palace Museum, Taipei; **63-65** AA/Mireille Vautier;
66t Lonely Planet Images/Krzysztof Dydynski; **66b** Corbis/Kevin
Fleming; **67t** AA/British Museum; **67b** WFA/Private Collection; **69** LPC;
71 AA; **72** Lonely Planet Images/Krzysztof Dydynski; **75** Corbis/Mike
McQueen; **76-77** Corbis/Pierre Colombel; **78l** Corbis/Tibor Bognar;
78r Corbis/JAI/Demetrio Carrasco; **79t** Lonely Planet Images/Krzysztof
Dydynski; **79b** Corbis/John Slater; **81** BAL/Oriental Museum, Durham
University; **82-83** Scala Archives/HIP/British Library; **85** BAL;
87 Corbis/Asian Art & Archaeology, Inc.; **88** WFA/Christian Deydier;
89 WFA/Private Collection